STARTING YOUR URBAN CSA

A Step-by-Step Guide
to Creating a
Community-Supported
Agriculture Project in
Your Urban Neighborhood

Produced by the Enright Ridge Urban E—
the support of a grant from the John A. Sc—

STARTING YOUR URBAN CSA

*A Step-by-Step Guide to Creating
a Community-Supported Agriculture Project
in Your Urban Neighborhood*

Published in the United States of America
by Bold Face Press, an imprint of the Price Hill Historical Society

Enright Ridge Urban EcoVillage CSA
www.enright-csa.org

Contents

Chapter 5   Growing Your Produce   51

Chapter 6   Distributing Your Produce   63

Preface

I started thinking about organizing an urban CSA in my community more than 25 years ago. In 2009 it finally happened, when the Enright Ridge CSA was established as part of the farm project of the Enright Ridge Urban EcoVillage, where I live. We received a grant to buy an abandoned greenhouse and florist shop on our street, spent the late winter cleaning and repairing the building, and had seeds in the ground by April. The first year we had a fairly small group, but we all worked hard, and under the supervision of an experienced farmer and an AmeriCorps administrator, the CSA thrived.

Every year we've gotten a little bigger, and for several years we had other AmeriCorps workers who learned about high production farming from our expert while they helped raise the crops for the CSA. We use successive plantings in the same bed and high-volume production techniques, and in our second year we were providing produce for more than 100 people (about 45 shares) for six months of the year on less than an acre of land in total. In our third year, we expanded with additional land in another community a few miles away that allowed us to grow a wider variety of crops, but we also experienced a drought that summer that was a major challenge. We still had plenty of produce, however, and the number of shares continued to grow.

By the third season, we knew we wanted to share what we had learned about urban co-op farming, and we applied for a grant to write this manual. It's taken another couple of seasons to get everything we know into words, but we think it's been worth the time and effort it has taken. We have changed and improved our processes every season, so it is an ongoing learning process, but we believe other neighborhoods can learn from our experience—our missteps and our successes.

It's my dream that someday every neighborhood in Cincinnati, every neighborhood across the country and around the world, will all have flourishing urban farms. It's time to learn how to feed ourselves again, and we want to encourage you to give it a try. If an urban co-operative community-supported agriculture project is right for your neighborhood, we hope what we've learned can help you over some of the hurdles and smooth your path. If you have a smaller—or bigger—project in mind, you might still find some useful information in these pages. From a backyard victory garden to a community vegetable patch to a full-fledged urban farm business, we want to see people all over the world growing their own food in their own neighborhoods. It's a good thing to do—for our health and economy and for the future of our planet.

If you would like further consultation around setting up a CSA, don't hesitate to contact us, by email at info@enright-csa.org or by mail at P.O. Box 5206, Cincinnati, OH 45205.

For Earth!

Jim Schenk

April 2013

Acknowledgments

Not long after the Enright Ridge CSA was up and running, Jim Schenk knew he wanted to share what was being learned and experienced with a larger audience. He really does envision a day when every neighborhood in every city has a sustainable urban farm project helping to feed its residents. So, this manual has been an important part of our urban CSA almost from the beginning.

The project was a major undertaking, and it took some hard work and long hours by many people. We would like to thank the people and organizations that made it possible to research, write, and publish this guide to starting your own urban CSA, including

Farmers and assistants Charles Griffin, Jeri Nakamura, Dave Rudemiller, Dave Hill, Heather Sayre, and Katie Burnside, for their expertise in keeping the farm project moving forward and for sharing that expertise,

University of Cincinnati students Shirley Yip and Peter Arioso, for their excellent research, and their professor, Rebecca Borah, for suggesting urban farming as a topic for research,

Nancy Sullivan, for the photographs she has taken documenting the urban farm project, many of which are used in this manual,

Christine Boatwright, for assistance with the grant proposal that made this manual possible,

Leeann Garrett, for her help and support in the initial stages of the project,

The grant received from the John A. Schroth Family Charitable Trust that made the writing and publishing of this manual possible,

Cyrus Flanders, the manuscript's first reader, for his attention to detail, which resulted in his catching redundancies and unintended errors,

Erich Kerby, who proofread the pages and caught typographic errors and mistakes that those of us who had read it too many times had missed,

And all the Enright Ridge CSA members over the past five years who have worked hard to create a vibrant and sustainable urban agriculture project in our neighborhood, Price Hill.

Introduction

When tillage begins, other arts follow.
Farmers are the founders
of human civilization.
—Daniel Webster

WHAT IS AN URBAN CSA?

Community-supported agriculture (CSA) is way of sustaining farming and farmers by ensuring that a farmer has a market for his crops. Consumers who are interested in safe, wholesome, locally grown food come together to support a farm operation, creating a community farm in which all the "shareholders" share the risks and benefits of food production on a local level.

The Enright Ridge CSA is urban because it is entirely within the city limits of Cincinnati, Ohio. It began in February 2009 as project of the Enright Ridge Urban EcoVillage (ERUEV), a community of people who are dedicated to sustainable living in an urban neighborhood called Price Hill, not far from downtown Cincinnati. The ERUEV promotes social and economic well-being while contributing to the preservation of our planet. Its residents are building a new way of life on the foundations of a beautiful historic area with affordable homes, acres of forest that surround the ridge, and a traditionally strong sense of community to create a safe, healthy, and ecologically sound neighborhood.

The ERUEV has been working for years to create a sustainable city neighborhood, and the urban farm project is part of that vision. It is headquartered at a former florist's greenhouse near the EcoVillage, but the CSA is also open to anyone in the Cincinnati area who is interested in helping to grow food locally.

CSAs take many forms, and the Enright Ridge CSA farm project was established as a work co-operative, with

The Enright Urban EcoVillage is a sustainable living project in Cincinnati, Ohio

members sharing the work of growing food in backyards and the community. We currently grow produce more than six months a year and provide food for approximately 200 people with garden and farm plots that add up to about an acre of land.

Members pay a fee and agree to work a minimum number of hours during the year for a share of the bounty from May to October (though we do also have some nonwork shares). The CSA grows a variety of produce, including many kinds of greens and herbs, eggplant, tomatoes, beets, carrots, peppers, beans, broccoli, cabbage, garlic, potatoes, squash, and more. Member shares are available for pickup every Saturday morning during the growing season at the greenhouse, which serves as a distribution center as well as a plant nursery.

CSA members work with the farm staff to grow produce in several plots of land that make up the urban farm (PHOTO: ERUEV)

We continue to grow, adding more land and more members. Our goal is to continue our own success with this community-based urban agriculture project while working to develop a network that will encourage other communities in Cincinnati and elsewhere to create their own CSAs.

That is why we have created this manual, so we can share our successes and the knowledge we have acquired over the several years our CSA has been in operation. We would like to see CSAs in every neighborhood across the country. This manual will help you get a CSA started in your own part of the world.

HOW AN URBAN CSA DIFFERS FROM OTHER KINDS OF CSAS

An urban co-op CSA like Enright Ridge is unique for several reasons:

- ▶ We grow our produce in small plots in an urban setting.
- ▶ We're a co-operative, member-supported organization with a professional farm staff.
- ▶ We are an outgrowth of an established ecovillage in the area.
- ▶ We operate as a nonprofit.
- ▶ Our intensive farm production methods have helped make our urban CSA successful.

The main thing that distinguishes our CSA is that it represents a group effort to grow food sustainably with limited resources. That is, our land and finances are limited, but we have discovered that our members provide us with an almost endless source of other types of resources.

Rather than depending on one farmer and one farm (at a distance from our urban homes) to provide us with food during the growing season, we've taken the initiative to grow our own food, right here in the city. We believe that our strength is in the members who make up the CSA and contribute their work hours, as well as a dedicated core committee that guides the project and a hard-working staff of farmers who organize and oversee our farm plots. This co-operative approach is what sets us apart and what we think is worth sharing.

WHAT'S IN THIS MANUAL

Our main goal in creating this manual is to present our vision of the future in food production that brings farming back to the local level. Our CSA model is oriented toward training more farmers to help establish many neighborhood CSAs that will involve the people who benefit from the produce being grown in their communities.

The manual, as well as additional references provided, will guide you through the steps involved in starting a successful urban CSA. The text is divided into chapters that cover the basics of running a successful CSA:

Chapter 1: Is an Urban Co-op CSA Right for Your Neighborhood? This chapter provides some thoughtful discussion of how to decide if an urban farm project will be successful in your community. It explains the urban co-operative model of farming and also gives examples of other types of CSAs.

Chapter 2: Finding Sites for Your CSA If you are going to farm, you need a place to grow plants. Those areas where you plan to grow need some basic amenities, such as water. You also need a

Tending early crops planted in our greenhouse, which also allows us to start seedlings for succession planting, discussed in more detail in Chapter 5

Copyright © 2013 Enright Ridge Urban EcoVillage CSA

place or a method for starting seedlings, a place to distribute what you grow, and you may need to consider zoning and land value issues.

Chapter 3: Finding People to Join Your CSA After you have a place for your CSA, you need members to make it work. This chapter gives some advice on how to recruit members and what motivates people to become part of an urban CSA. There is also information about how to determine share sizes and pricing, how to retain the members who join, and how to determine if members are satisfied with the CSA.

Chapter 4: The Business Side: Manging and Financing Your CSA It's not all about growing the produce; you will also need people who are proficient at managing a complex operation, as well as people who are skilled at finding startup and operating funds. This chapter also covers staffing, coordinating volunteers, creating budgets, and insurance and liability issues.

Chapter 5: Growing Your Produce Now to the meat of the matter—or the vegetables, more precisely. This chapter gives an overview of production methods and provides many resources that can help you plan, plant, and reap the bounty that your members will enjoy. Other topics covered include soil and bed preparation, irrigation and pest control, composting, harvesting, and tools and equipment.

Chapter 6: Distributing Your Produce The final step is getting the produce you've grown to your members. You need to organize a place and a schedule for members to pick up their share of the harvest, and you need the produce to be prepared following GAP (Good Agriculture Practices) and food safety guidelines. You also need to have a set policy for members to follow when picking up their produce to make it equally convenient for those preparing the produce and those picking it up.

Chapter 7: Communications You will need to keep in touch with your members; in a co-operative CSA, this is especially important, because you need members to be available for work assignments as well as keeping them abreast of information about what is being harvested. Electronic communication, such as a website and social media, is almost mandatory, but you can also use traditional methods of communication to get the word out.

Chapter 8: Beyond the Farm When you are ready to start signing up members and growing your first crops, there are a few odds and ends you'll need to consider. This chapter also provides information about the long-range effects of starting an urban CSA—how it can establish value chains of support services that can lead to community building and even job creation.

At the end of the manual, there are forms that you can use for planning your urban CSA and a bibliography of print and electronic resources for reference.

STARTING YOUR OWN URBAN CSA— WHY WOULD YOU WANT TO?

This manual provides step-by-step guidance to start your own urban, co-operative CSA. We want to encourage people everywhere to start community-supported urban agriculture projects. People need to reconnect with the earth and with the food supply it provides. Food doesn't come from

Supermarket produce often lacks variety and most of it travels a long way from field to store

CSA members enjoy a variety of fresh local produce, including some they may never have tried before

grocery stores; it comes from seeds and soil and sun, and the gap between food production and food consumption has caused serious problems in our society. There is a need in our world today to work toward more local sources for food.

The Leopold Center for Sustainable Agriculture in Iowa produced a study titled "Food, Fuel, and Freeways" that used U.S. Department of Agriculture data to find out how far produce traveled to what is termed a terminal market, where brokers and wholesalers buy produce to sell to grocery stores and restaurants. The results of the study were not surprising to the researchers, but it might startle you to learn that "fresh" produce in the United States travels an average of 1,400 miles to market!

DIG DEEPER

Study results were reported by the Center for Urban Education about Sustainable Agriculture (CUESA) http:// www.cuesa.org/page/how-far-does-your-food-travel-get-your-plate.

During World War II, food and other consumer goods were rationed as part of the war effort. The government encouraged people to plant Victory Gardens, to provide food locally for their own families so that many products—not just food, but also fuel and rubber used for truck tires, both needed to move food from farms to customers—could be conserved. Such practices came easily to people who had lived through a major economic depression in the previous decade. But after the war, there was a turnaround. Industries wanted to maintain and increase their markets, and consumerism—buying rather than producing what your family needed—became more common and was encouraged through advertising. We have been trained to be overly consumptive as a matter of personal and national pride, but it is time for another change, to become producers again, not just consumers.

New York City had dairy and vegetable farms within its urban area through the late 19th and early 20th centuries. Cities like Paris had sustainable agriculture more than a century ago. The "French-intensive" method of growing vegetables by adding large amounts of compost annually to densely planted raised beds—was developed in the crowded inner-city neighborhoods (the arrondissements) of 19th century Paris. It is time we all started thinking about where our food comes from and how it is grown.

For more current examples, we might turn to the urban farms sprouting up on abandoned properties around Detroit, and Will Allen's Growing Power operations in Milwaukee and Chicago. The benefits of locally grown food are many:

DIG DEEPER

Find out more about Will Allen's urban farm projects at www.growingpower.org and see the video *Urban Roots* to learn more about inner-city agriculture in Detroit (www.urbanrootsamerica.com).

▶ Fresh food is healthier and helps people make connections among available food, diet, and nutrition.

▶ Instead of depending on grapes from Chile or tomatoes from Mexico, you eat what is in season in your area—radishes and turnips and greens in May, strawberries and kale in June, tomatoes and squash in August. You can buy peaches in December, but consider the hidden costs of transporting those peaches 5,000 miles or more from South America to Ohio. Members of a CSA enjoy eating well and have the satisfaction of knowing what they eat has been grown locally and sustainably.

▶ You can extend the season for eating local food by learning to can, dry, and freeze the produce that comes in abundantly during the growing season, preserving it to eat during the winter months.

▶ Members also have the opportunity to learn new farm and garden methods, tool use, and greenhouse operation, as well as skills in composting, harvesting, pest management, and soil and bed preparation.

▶ Other benefits of membership in a CSA include fostering a sense of community through social events, developing a newsletter and using social media to share recipes and information about preparing, preserving, and storing the produce.

WHO IS THIS MANUAL FOR?

This project, which includes a manual, a training program for farmers, and consultation assistance for neighborhoods contemplating the establishment of their own urban CSAs, is intended for people living in urban areas who are interested in working together to establish a strong community through locally grown food.

People in urban areas have a unique opportunity to pursue agricultural projects that use efficient and highly productive methods to create sustainable gardens to feed themselves and their neighbors. Working co-operatively, this is an achievable goal.

If you want to eat better, save money, get healthier, live more sustainably, help your local economy, and make a positive impact in your community, think about starting an urban CSA. It offers more value for your food dollar, because the food moves directly from the farm or garden to the consumer. All the middlemen and extra costs—the costs of shipping, the added profits of brokers and retailers, the salaries of lobbyists for big agricultural interests—disappear if you grow your own food in or near your own neighborhood.

The food you receive will be fresher than anything you get at a supermarket, and the selection will be more diverse, too. Over the course of the season, a CSA farm usually grows more types of vegetables than found at a grocery store. You'll have the chance to try vegetables and varieties that you might not otherwise find or buy, from leeks and celeriac to daikon and bok choi. You'll find out just how tasty some produce you've never heard of can be when it's fresh and well prepared.

So, the answer is—this manual is for you, when you decide that growing fresh food in your urban neighborhood is the answer to how to help your community thrive. You'll eat better, and the result is a noticeable improvement in your own well-being and the well-being of your community.

WHY DID WE CREATE THIS MANUAL?

The Enright Ridge CSA was no more than a dream of one of the EcoVillage members for more than two decades. When a greenhouse in the neighborhood became available and a professional farmer made his home in the EcoVillage, it seemed like the time was finally right. The CSA has been growing every year, and it has garnered a lot of local publicity. People want to learn how to grow their own food and so we want to help other neighborhoods start successful community-supported agriculture projects.

There was a learning curve for us as we got the operation up and running, and now we want to share what we've learned to make the process easier for people in other neighborhoods. Our hope is that one CSA will lead to another and another and another . . . until every neighborhood has people who are growing their own food.

HOW TO USE THIS MANUAL AND ITS RESOURCES

We kept this manual short intentionally; there are some aspects of starting and maintaining a CSA that apply no matter where you are and what you grow. But there are also a lot of facets that will be unique to your community and your group. We can't provide an exact blueprint of how every new CSA will be organized, nor could we expect that simply giving you the details of our urban farm project will cover everything you

need to know. Instead, we provide an overview of the main steps in starting and running a co-operative CSA, with links and references to point you to more. There are electronic and print resources that will tell you much more about the crops that are suited for your area, for example; you can also refer to knowledgeable sources for more information about soil testing, zoning regulations, and financial guidelines that are applicable to your community and your situation.

We've included some illustrations and tables to give you information in a visual way, and also have included sample forms and charts in an appendix that you may find useful for planning.

Take advantage of all the outside resources you need to find information suited to your

Growing fresh food in your urban neighborhood is good for your health and good for the community

situation, with this manual as your advisor. The Enright Ridge CSA staff and committee members are also available to answer specific questions and provide consulting services. We are committed to the idea of urban farming, and someday we would like to see a successful CSA in every city neighborhood.

Now it's time to take the first step, deciding if an urban co-op CSA is right for your neighborhood. There are other types of community-supported agriculture you might also consider, but whatever path you follow, we wish you good luck and great food in your future. ■

DIG DEEPER

Contact the Enright Ridge CSA by e-mail at info@enright-csa.org.

Chapter 1

Is an Urban Co-op CSA Right for Your Neighborhood?

*Farming looks mighty easy when
your plow is a pencil and you're
a thousand miles from the corn.*

—*Dwight D. Eisenhower*

If you and other people in your community have begun questioning your food sources, preferring to buy fresh food from seasonal or established farmers' markets, or have been lamenting the lack of fresh produce near where you live, it's time to start thinking about starting (or at least joining) a community-supported agriculture project.

A SHORT HISTORY OF CO-OPERATIVE FARMING

CSAs first appeared in the 1960s in Europe, when farmers and customers formed co-operative partnerships that were designed to provide financial support that would allow farmers to grow their crops using ecological and sustainable practices. The co-operatives were also inspired by economic ideas of social equity, with a goal of providing safe and healthy food to as many people as possible.

In Japan, a group of mothers concerned about the decreasing number of farms and farmers and the increasing amount of imported food began forming farming collectives called *teikei*, which translates as "co-operative."

The idea of co-operative farming came to the United States in the mid-1980s. The term *community-supported agriculture* was coined to describe a co-operative farm project that began in New Hampshire at that time, and in the past three decades, thousands of such farms have been organized in the United States and Canada. Though most of them are in rural or semi-rural areas, CSAs have become increasingly popular in urban areas. Intensive farming methods that require small plots of land to grow a reasonable amount of produce have made the urban CSA is a great idea whose time has arrived.

Communal farming is not a new idea—for millennia, people around the world have worked together to raise the food they need to survive (DETAIL FROM *FLEMISH DAIRY*, JAN BRUEGHEL; PRADO MUSEUM, MADRID)

The Urban Co-operative Model

An urban CSA provides the opportunity to grow our own food literally in our own backyards. A well-designed CSA in an urban community can produce a significant amount of food in a relatively small area using a professional farmer. The food will be high quality—organic if you choose—and the model provides a chance to "get your hands dirty" growing the food you eat. It can also serve as an economic engine and a way to build community cohesiveness, providing employment to a farmer and sometimes other staff, and creating a bond between neighbors who work together farming.

There are a lot of great reasons to start an urban CSA, but it is also a lot of hard work. You are building a farm literally from the ground up, in an area that may not have had farming activity in decades. And you won't just be farming—you will also be developing a business, and to be successful, you must run it as a business. However, as a co-operative, the members own the business, and they are committed to its success.

WHAT'S THE BUZZ

Research shows that 20 to 30 shares per acre is reasonable, but it is possible to grow more with intensive farming techniques—as much as 40 or 50 shares per acre.

STARTING YOUR URBAN CSA

As with any business, you will face challenges setting up an urban CSA—but there will be benefits as well. You must think about the resources you have, the resources you need, and the resources you can acquire—land, water, seeds, and tools, but also experience, committed members, and financial support. Some of the challenges will include:

▶ Selecting a suitable location, near your potential shareholders and with enough arable land, access to water, and a potential distribution site

▶ Diverse crop production—growing as many as 30 different kinds of greens and vegetables—to provide shareholders with a variety of produce throughout the growing season

▶ Ensuring there is adequate labor to accomplish the farming, distribution, and management tasks including planting, tending, harvesting, cleaning, and distribution of crops every week

▶ Identifying volunteers with skills to assist in the business-side tasks, such as managing the finances, recruiting and retaining members, and setting up channels of communication

You will see some benefits from an urban CSA immediately, and others will emerge over the years:

▶ Members share fresh, healthy food grown sustainably in their own neighborhood

▶ One or more farmers (and apprentice farmers) will be gainfully employed in your community

▶ Financial risks of the farm and the business are shared among many people

▶ Relationships form between members, encouraging a sense of community and building a stronger neighborhood

WHAT'S THE BUZZ

Start small and grow slowly to ensure that your limited resources can efficiently grow enough produce to satisfy your members. Starting small also makes it easier to manage the volunteer labor of members doing the work on the farm and handling the business and management tasks.

In some CSAs, the farmer makes all of the production and business decisions—the shareholders pay for their share at the beginning of the season, and then their only responsibility is picking up their produce on distribution days. An urban co-op CSA asks more of its members, who are involved in decision making and must assist in many of the tasks that keep the farm going. Now it's time to start planning.

PLANNING YOUR CSA

Before you begin to develop your CSA plan consider these questions: How will you take advantage of the resources unique to your community—personnel and natural resources? What challenges will you face? How is your community/your market different from others, and how can you leverage these differences to your advantage? Are there currently enough/varied alternatives for purchasing fresh and local food nearby?

You also need to think about the financial and business side of the CSA: What are your financial goals, sources of funding, and potential member pool? Estimate your annual operating costs as you plan. Do you have potential leadership personnel as well as people to turn to with the farming ability, marketing skills, financial know-how, and other specialties required to set up a successful urban CSA?

Ten Planning Steps for an Urban Co-op CSA

1. Even though it is a co-operative, one or two people must take the initiative and be the point person(s) for the project. This person or persons will be the driving force to make it happen. Eventually, a lead committee or core group will form to direct the CSA, but that committee requires leadership.

2. Developing the CSA requires a relatively long-term commitment. The Enright Ridge CSA was unusual in that we were up and running within a six-month period, but it has taken several seasons to get it working at full strength. Over the years, the leadership may change, but it will be an ongoing necessity. We have learned that the farmers do not have the time and energy to both farm and do the day-to-day work of running the CSA. There are many things members can do to help in the success of the CSA. These co-operative tasks are mentioned briefly here and will be covered in more depth in following chapters of this manual.

3. Having a committee to work on the project is important. Unless there is someone willing to spend half to full time creating the CSA, a committee will be needed to plan and organize.

4. One of the first tasks is to find land. There are backyards, fields, and vacant lots spread throughout our cities that can be used to grow food with a reasonable amount of preparation. Identifying these places and gaining access to using them is a high priority. See Chapter 2, "Finding Sites for Your CSA," for more about this topic.

Farmers at work transplanting early spring seedlings in the Enright CSA greenhouse (PHOTO: JIM SCHENK)

5. Finding a farmer is also critical. There is a shortage of farmers who have experience with urban CSAs, so it will be challenging to find someone (and this position will almost certainly be a paid employee), but the act of creating your urban CSA ensures that there are more opportunities for such farmers and will encourage more people to seek training for such jobs. The Enright Ridge CSA has been actively involved in creating a training and internship program for people who want to learn to be urban farmers as a way to help fill this gap. Chapter 4, "The Business Side: Financing and Managing Your CSA," has more about hiring farm staff.

6. Getting people to join the CSA as members is also high on the priority list. You need to determine how many members you can handle in the first year. This number will be determined by the amount of land, the availability and ability of the farmer, and the amount of funds you have to launch the CSA. Word of mouth is often the best place to start. You are enthusiastic about the project, and when you tell friends and family and encourage them to tell other people about the CSA, the word will get out. Chapter 3, "Finding People to Join Your CSA," will give you more ideas about how to recruit members.

7. More formal methods of communication are also important. Consider developing a brochure, creating a website, distributing fliers, and having articles published about the project in local newspapers to spread the word. You also need to keep in touch with members. Chapter 7, "Communications," provides additional information about how to market your CSA and keep your current members informed of what's happening.

8. Like all new businesses, having sufficient capital to get started is helpful. It may take time for the CSA to reach the point of providing for itself. Money is an important resource, but there are also others. Some of the land, for instance, may be donated, or members may allow use of land they own for one or more seasons. Free sources of compost for enriching the soil may be available, and vehicles may be donated to carry materials. Other CSAs may be able to provide resources like greenhouse space. Some people may want to volunteer their time to work as farmers, or members may be willing to provide equipment. Many resources may be out there that do not require an outlay of money. However, funds *will* be needed to get the CSA underway. You will need to pay the farmer (unless the farmer is willing to volunteer his or her time), buy seeds and fertilizer, and buy or rent some equipment. It is important to have a budget, a bank account, someone who understands finances, and insurance. Chapter 4, "The Business Side: Financing and Managing Your CSA," goes into more detail about the financial and managerial side of the CSA.

9. Determining the type of food to be grown is also an important task. Although introducing some new foods can be exciting, the majority of the crops you grow should be familiar items that members want to cook and eat. It's important to involve members in planning in a significant way. Chapter 5, "Growing Your Produce," talks more about planning what to grow, and Chapter 3, "Finding People to Join Your CSA" has some tips on how to survey members.

10. You also need to work out how and where the CSA will distribute the food it grows. You may use a public facility or set up in a member's garage. There are also questions to consider about how to display the food, whether it is sold by weight or item, and if it is packed in advance or members will pack their own shares. You also have to think about how and where to store the food between harvest and distribution. Chapter 6, "Distributing the Produce," will help you determine how to approach many of these logistical problems.

Think these issues through thoroughly as you consider the decision to start your own CSA.

OTHER MODELS

Although this book is about urban co-operative agriculture projects, there is no set way to organize a CSA. Think of community-supported farming as a frame—the picture within the frame can change drastically, but generally speaking, it's always art. In the same way, calling something a CSA is a way to frame the discussion and inspire communities to work together with local farmers to create sustainable food options where they live.

First let's take a look at what you might want your CSA to do for you. A community-supported agriculture project could . . .

> . . . grow vegetables in yards and hoop houses to supply a weekly box of produce for members throughout the year

> . . . help run an established organic farm and support the farm's shop or produce stand

> . . . sponsor the care and maintenance of an established orchard or vineyard and share in the harvest of its fruit

> . . . rent a plot of land, enlist the services of a farmer, and have her grow vegetables on your behalf

> . . . create a collaborative with a local bakery, dairy farmer, and poultry farmer to receive a regular supply of eggs, cheese, and bread

> . . . and almost limitless other possibilities!

Community-supported agriculture can take many different forms, including supporting an established vineyard or orchard to promote permaculture in your area

Common methods of organizing community-supported agriculture projects include

▶ Farmer-driven, or farmer co-operative CSAs, organized and run by entrepreneurial farmers

▶ Community or consumer-organized gardens

▶ Church- or school-sponsored farms or gardens

Entrepreneurial Farmer CSAs

The most traditional form of CSA involves a farmer with land who produces vegetables and other food products for a group of committed members who pay for their share of the bounty in advance, providing stability and financial support for agriculture in your community and sharing the risks inherent in farming among all of the members, including the farmer.

Most commonly, they are organized by the farmer, who sells subscriptions. In its most structured form, such an operation has a common-pricing system based on an established budget, so the farmer's costs are covered, she earns a reasonable wage for her work, and the risks and rewards of farming are shared. That is, the members do not pay directly per pound of produce, but instead pay a set price in advance and receive a share of as much (or as little) as the farm produces each week of what is ready to harvest.

This approach eliminates the need for the farmer to market her goods and thus saves time and labor, allowing the farmer to focus on quality care of the soils and crops and serving customers by producing a good variety of food that people want to eat. It provides financial stability for the farmer based on thorough planning and a well-conceived budget. There were more than 15,000 CSAs in the United States and Canada in 2010, and the majority of them are based on this kind of model.

DIG DEEPER

In the Cincinnati area, there are many traditional CSAs, many of them listed in the Central Ohio River Valley (CORV) food guide, at www.eatlocalcorv.org.

Community or Civic Gardens

A community garden is a single piece of land gardened collectively by a group of people. Community gardens provide fresh produce and give participants a sense of accomplishment through their labor in growing and harvesting the crops. They also create a connection to the environment and can promote community building and neighborhood improvement. Some community gardens are owned jointly by their members, others are owned and leased by local governments, and some are held in trust and managed by nonprofit associations.

Community gardens can vary widely, from small Victory Gardens with plots of common vegetables, to minimal street beautification planters on urban street corners, to extensive projects intended to preserve

Hillside Community Garden (www.hillsidegardendelhi.com) at Mt. St. Joseph College in suburban Cincinnati has created an informal community garden where anyone who volunteers to help can share in the bounty (PHOTO: AMY MATTHEWS STROSS/HILLSIDE COMMUNITY GARDEN)

natural areas. In England, a former Victorian mill town in Yorkshire called Todmorden uses every bit of public space to grow food. There are apple trees along the old canal towpath, carrots and kale growing in raised beds in front of the police department, beans and peas planted on the college green, and cherries and raspberries surrounding the supermarket parking lot. People help themselves to what they want; there is no organized distribution. And so far it has worked out fine—the townspeople have found that, at least in Todmorden, people are decent and only take what they can use.

DIG DEEPER

Read more about the Todmorden experiment in growing food in public spaces at http://www.dailymail.co.uk/femail/ article-2072383/Eccentric-town-Todmorden-growing-ALL-veg.html.

Community gardens can bring out the best in people, and they also go a long way in improving the planet. They can help alleviate one effect of climate change, which is expected to cause a global decline in agricultural output, making fresh produce increasingly unaffordable. Community gardens create a sense of food security in urban communities, and locally grown food decreases reliance on fossil fuels to transport food from large agribusiness farms; it also reduces use of fossil fuels to drive agricultural machinery on those huge corporate farms.

Then there are the health benefits of community gardens, the driving force behind organizations such as Closing the Health Gap in Cincinnati (_http://closingthehealthgap.org_). By encouraging community gardens in inner-city neighborhoods, nonprofits such as these encourage people to eat better, consuming the fresh vegetables they have grown themselves, and also provides a form of exercise for the people doing the gardening. Neighborhoods that work together on community projects like gardens also experience less crime and vandalism. A report on the benefits of community gardens is available online (_http://www.communitygarden.org/docs/learn/articles/ multiple_benefits.pdf_).

WHAT'S THE BUZZ

The Civic Garden Center of Cincinnati (www.civicgardencenter.org) lists community gardens they sponsor and offers help in starting new community gardens in the area.

In Detroit, Chicago, Milwaukee, and other American cities, vacant lots and abandoned areas in neighborhoods have been turned into productive gardens. In other towns, community gardens are regarded as a recreational amenity and are included in public parks. Some community gardens are worked collectively, with everyone pitching in to grow crops that they then share; others are split into clearly divided plots, each managed by a different gardener (or group or family).

Church- or School-Sponsored Farms and Gardens

Church- and school-sponsored gardens are similar to community gardens, and in some cases these types overlap. For instance, Closing the Health Gap in Cincinnati has worked with the community of Avondale to establish a community garden behind a local church, and church members are among the most enthusiastic customers of the farmers' market run by community garden members, many of whom are school children.

Schools present a particularly good opportunity to introduce community farming. Students, directed by teachers or volunteers, learn not only how to grow their own food, but also form a connection to the earth

Dater Montessori School's Nature Center (https://www.facebook.com/DaterNatureCenter) uses vegetable gardens to educate students about the cycle of life as well as healthy eating habits (Photo: Susan VonderHaar, Dater Montessori Nature Center)

and establish healthy eating habits. Dater Montessori School in Westwood, a Cincinnati neighborhood, has vegetable gardens, cold frames, native plant gardens, a butterfly garden, and an arboretum. Students who participate in a summer nature program at the school raise a variety of vegetables in raised beds and learn how to prepare what they grow when it is harvested.

State standards for education include many requirements for hands-on learning, and activities like gardening allow students to learn practical applications of lessons in science, health, and social studies. Any school with a little land around the building can encourage a lifelong connection with the earth by creating gardens and producing food sustainably. In some places, school gardens have become so large and productive that they actually supply the food used for school lunches.

Other Options

Someday we want to see a CSA in every neighborhood across the United States. But realistically, we know everyone isn't ready to start their own CSA, or even begin community gardening tomorrow. There are other options:

▶ Join an existing CSA

▶ Shop at farmers' markets

▶ Investigate fresh food delivery services

DIG DEEPER

Find out more about the Alice Waters School Lunch Initiative—known as the Edible Schoolyard Project—at http://edibleschoolyard.org.

You could join an existing CSA today (or at least at the beginning of the next growing season). There are CSAs in our area, but there are far fewer *urban* CSAs—most are in rural and suburban areas. Still, it's much easier to find a CSA than to start your own. In fact, if you are planning to start a CSA, we encourage you to join one first, to see how it works. This is a good idea, but not a necessity—when we started the Enright Ridge CSA, none of the original organizers had belonged to a CSA, but with hindsight we believe it would have been helpful if we had experienced one firsthand.

Alternately, you can begin buying more of your food from farmers' markets. Here in Cincinnati, we are lucky to have an urban jewel called Findlay Market (www.findlaymarket.org), located in the historic Over the Rhine neighborhood. Findlay Market is more than 150 years old; it was established through a bequest from General James Findlay to the city of Cincinnati to establish a market house. The original market house still stands (though it received a major renovation a few years ago), housing independent merchants who

Cincinnati's Findlay Market supports small businesses and local growers with fresh food choices year round and a farmers' market during the growing season

sell meat, cheese, seafood, spices, and other products. Area farmers set up stands around the market house to sell produce in season. In addition to Findlay Market, the CORV Food Guide (*http://www.eatlocalcorv.org*) can provide you with information about dozens of other farmers' markets in the Cincinnati area, and many other communities also have directories of farmers' markets online.

Or you might want to try ordering food from a company like Green Bean Delivery that purchases local and (sometimes) organic food and boxes it up for their customers. Even supermarkets have begun to label food that is produced locally, so with some care and forethought, you can choose to buy local and sustainably produced food from traditional sources.

All of these options existed when we began the Enright Ridge CSA, but we realized they didn't provide the same sense of ownership, of hands-on involvement, of truly working toward expanding sustainable local food sources. If the amount of work it takes to set up a CSA does not deter you, then we encourage you to "go for it"—start your own urban co-operative farm. ▪

Chapter 2

Finding Sites for Your CSA

Though the land be good,
you cannot have an abundant crop
without cultivation.

—Plato

U rban agriculture is becoming increasingly popular in the United States. There is a growing local food movement and people are interested in more sustainable communities within cities. Community gardening is the most popular form of urban agriculture, with many neighborhoods setting aside a vacant lot or area in a public park for citizens to garden and grow vegetables.

Finding land to grow vegetables for a self-sufficient urban CSA requires a little more ingenuity, but it's not an insurmountable hurdle. Older industrial cities including Buffalo, Cleveland, and Detroit have emerged as hotbeds of urban agriculture because they have increasing amounts of vacant land as their populations declined drastically. Smaller populations and more available land have put these cities on the leading edge of changes in food production, and the citizens of these cities are experimenting with going back to becoming producers, not just consumers.

Because urban agriculture requires land that is often zoned and regulated for specific uses, the increase in farming within cities has implications for municipal planning. Sustainable communities thrive with less or no zoning, allowing people to work, live, play, and produce food in one place without commuting. Our dream is that within the city limits of Cincinnati, there will be a large number of CSAs developed that will allow residents of urban neighborhoods to grow food near where they live and work.

The geology of the valley and hillsides of Cincinnati leaves large swathes of "unimproved" land, because the unstable rock formations that form the city's hills necessitate that we not build close to the slopes. Also, there were once a half million people living in the city, but now the population is under 300,000. Many houses are vacant, and many have already been torn down. In the suburbs, homes often have large backyards that are ideal for growing food for a CSA.

FINDING LAND TO FARM

A CSA requires about one acre of land to grow food for 30 to 40 subscriptions, although using high-yield methods of farming and a succession of crops in the same beds, an acre may be able to support up to 100 members. You'll need another acre or more for crops that require a lot of space, such as corn, squash, and potatoes. An acre is roughly 42,000 square feet. To give you an idea of the amount of space we're talking about, an acre is an area of land about 200 feet by 200 feet piece of land, or eleven typical suburban backyards, about 60 feet by 60 feet.

DIG DEEPER

Yield statistics are from www.CSAFarms.org, Community Supported Agriculture in Michigan.

You need sunlight, of course—backyards with heavy tree cover are not optimal sites for farming, but every neighborhood has open space that gets enough sun to grow crops. In Cincinnati, many city neighborhoods are lucky to have a lot of tree cover, which is good for the environment, provides shade in the summer, and makes the streets inviting. But even with all of our trees, we have been able to find open areas that are suitable for agriculture.

Backyard Farmland

So, you don't need a lot of land, which may come as a surprise to people accustomed to seeing vast fields of wheat or corn growing for miles in rural areas. Urban farming typically gets more yield from smaller areas, with shorter crop cycles, using the same land to grow several different varieties of produce in one season.

We began our search for land by looking at people's backyards in our neighborhood. This provided us with all the land we needed for the first couple of years. When you are organizing an urban CSA, it makes sense that some of the people you bring together have land that they are willing to share. And conversely, it also makes sense to invite people who have land that can be farmed to join your CSA.

We have developed a contract we use with backyard neighbors that allows us to farm their land

When you are looking for land to farm in your neighborhood, sometimes you only need to look as far as your own (or your neighbor's) backyard (PHOTO: NANCY SULLIVAN)

STARTING YOUR URBAN CSA

in exchange for either CSA share cost or the amount of volunteer hours expected of members. Members generally do not expect remuneration beyond a break on the cost or number of volunteer hours required by a share, but you can make arrangements to provide other compensation agreeable to both the property owner and the CSA.

DIG DEEPER

See Appendix A, p. 103, for a copy of the contract we use for backyard farming.

Looking Farther Afield

After several years of growing food in our members' backyards and a community garden (all within a few blocks of each other), we learned that there was a larger plot of land available on a farm a few miles from Price Hill, in the Cincinnati neighborhood of Sayler Park. We have grown corn, squash, beans, peppers, eggplant, and potatoes on an acre of land at this location.

Don't be afraid to look outside your neighborhood if you need additional land. Be flexible and consider any available land if it is easily accessible and logistically feasible (that is, water is available, the size of the land makes it possible to grow more crops and a greater variety of produce, and the land can be used free or for a small rental fee).

Public and Semi-Public Land

Unused farmland near your community, public land, vacant lots—all are possibilities for growing food in or near where you live—just look around you (Photo: Nancy Sullivan)

The city of Cincinnati has a significant amount of vacant land that they own, and many other cities also are the owners of record for unused property within their borders. If there is city land in your neighborhood, talk to someone in the building or property department at city hall to see if the property is available for community gardening.

Other public entities, such as community housing authorities, also own land that may not be occupied currently. In Price Hill, the Cincinnati Metropolitan Housing Authority has a multi-acre piece of property where housing was razed; the Enright CSA is now farming that land. There are also several plots of land owned by a local land trust that were originally community gardens but are not currently used.

Another possibility is checking with your local school board; existing schools often have excess land around their buildings, and the school board may also own land that once was used for a school or that they are planning to build on eventually. Sometimes these kinds of groups can be persuaded to negotiate a short lease on good terms to build community goodwill, with the understanding that when they want to develop the land, the farm will have to give up cultivation. But being able to use the land for a few years is well worth investigating, if the price is right and water is available.

Vacant land is often an eyesore in neighborhoods, and if the owner is willing to allow the land to be used for farming, it can improve the area, make the street safer, and even involve nearby residents.

Whenever you are negotiating to use property owned by the city or county, another entity, or a private owner, you should try to work out at least a three-year agreement to use the land. It usually will take at least a season to get the land in good condition for crop production, and being able to use it for at least a couple of years after it is functioning well gives your CSA the continuity it needs to produce well.

When you are talking to owners—public or private—about using vacant land for urban farming, you can make some good arguments for how such land use will improve the neighborhood and even potentially raise property values. New York University funded a study titled "The Effect of Community Gardens on Neighboring Property Values" that determined that community gardens create significant positive effects on surrounding property values. Those effects are positive across the board but inversely associated with current values in the neighborhood—that is, the poorest of host neighborhoods see the largest increase in value for surrounding property. The study also found that more organized and stable gardens—such as a co-operative CSA—have the greatest positive impact.

DIG DEEPER

The complete NYU study is available at http://onlinelibrary.wiley.com/doi/10.1111/j.1540-6229.2008.00213.x/abstract.

Purchasing Land

You may find that land suitable for farming is for sale in your community. If the price is right, purchasing it might make sense. Renting land, if the price is reasonable and the land is good, is also a possibility, and farming some of the semi-public land discussed previously sometimes involves paying a small lease fee. Also, you may find owners who are willing to donate their land for a good cause. It never hurts to ask!

You can find help concerning how to find land to farm online, though a lot of the information is geared more toward rural farming. But the information can be applicable to the purchase or lease of property anywhere. One guide, *The Field Guide for Beginning Farmers (http://fieldguideforbeginningfarmers.wikispaces.com/)*, talks about different ways to acquire land for crop production:

▶ Cash Lease   Most cash leases are short-term agreements with little commitment from either the landowner or the CSA. Though some leases are made on a handshake, it makes a lot more sense to get it in writing.

▶ Crop Share   This model is comparable to using members' backyards to grow CSA produce—the rent payment comes in the form of a share of what is grown.

▶ Long-term Lease   A long-term lease is almost the equivalent of ownership. Some leases can be for as long as 99 years, common with publicly owned land.

▶ Lease with Option to Buy   In this case, the land owner and the CSA negotiate a purchase price and agree on a date for purchase. A portion of the rent money paid from the time of agreement to the time of purchase is put toward the down payment for the land.

▶ Lease with Right of First Refusal   With this type of clause in a rental agreement, the landowner can only sell to a third party after the CSA has been notified and given a chance to match the offer.

▶ Purchase   Of course, you can always simply purchase the land, possibly with grant money—an urban CSA is not necessarily going to meet the qualifications for a bank mortgage. But there are many other possibilities, including seller financing, fundraising to purchase the land, and/or a sale at a very low price.

When you are looking for land to farm, the important thing is to keep your options open. When you find a space that looks promising, don't be afraid to explore it, find out who owns it, and see if it might be available and useful for your needs. There is a lot of available land around, even in urban settings—in Cincinnati's Over the Rhine neighborhood, which is in the inner city, there are about a half-dozen community gardens located on vacant lots, between buildings, and near the 160-year-old Findlay Market. The space you need is out there; find what will work for you.

GREENHOUSE FACILITIES

The main purpose of a greenhouse is to have a place to start seeds and grow seedlings until they are ready to be put out in the gardens. If you have a greenhouse in your CSA operation, you will need less land, because you will be able to have succession plantings in one garden. The Enright Ridge CSA has had up to five successions of plantings in a bed during the season, making the land we have extremely productive. However, if a greenhouse isn't available, there are other options, including starting seeds in cold frames or hoop houses, or seeds can be planted directly in the ground.

When we were forming our CSA, we found an article about setting up an urban farm project that argued a greenhouse was not needed during the first few years. For one thing, greenhouses take a lot of time to construct and to keep up.

We had the good fortune to have an abandoned greenhouse in the neighborhood. A florist had operated at the location for a hundred years, and the availability of the old greenhouse was a major impetus for starting the Enright Ridge CSA. We purchased the greenhouse and land for a very reasonable price, and more importantly, we received a grant to pay for the purchase and the needed renovations. So we have had a greenhouse from the start, and we have definitely benefited from having it—but for most urban CSAs, it is not essential for startup.

A greenhouse is a great asset, but it is not absolutely necessary for a startup CSA (Photo: ERUEV)

We used a much smaller greenhouse at the house of a nearby resident the first year, while our greenhouse was being repaired. If there is a greenhouse anywhere nearby, don't be afraid to ask if it can be used for the CSA.

Another option is to build a simple greenhouse, not a difficult task if you have people with carpentry skills. In an urban setting, however, construction of a greenhouse may require building permits. Hoop houses are another good option. They can be constructed or purchased relatively cheaply and do a very adequate job. Because they are temporary structures, there is less likelihood that you will need to apply for permits. One CSA in greater Cincinnati that has been in existence for many years uses only hoop houses.

DISTRIBUTION SPACE

It's a great day when your urban CSA begins to harvest produce, but there are some logistics you'll need to plan for before that day. When the harvest comes in, it needs to go out to members quickly. You will need to store the harvest as it comes in, and you'll need a place to distribute it to shareholders. One location for both storage and distribution works best, but if you do not have access to enough space to store all the food, or to a place that you can use to store it and distribute it, then consider how to operate with multiple spaces. Basements work fine for temporary crop storage. You can use a church, school, or other public facility in the neighborhood for distribution, especially if you arrange to use it on days when the facility's usual tenants are not there. You may be able to locate a decent-sized garden shed a neighborhood resident isn't using. Or you can construct a lean-to shed or hoop house as a distribution site.

After harvesting, distribution is a cleaner and simpler task if you have the facilities to wash the produce and volunteers available to do the work. But don't let this be a stumbling block—if you don't have a place or the people power to wash the vegetables before distributing them to shareholders, people can wash their own share at home. (There is more informa-

tion about pickup procedures in Chapter 6.)

Set up distribution so it works for you in the space you have. If the space is small, arrange staggered pickup times so that everyone doesn't arrive at the same time. If you have limited volunteers, set things up so people can come in and select their items from the harvest baskets. Alternatively, if you have limited space but plenty of help, pack up the food into shares ahead of time so that people can quickly pick up their box of food, or use several locations for share pickup. One member might get a quantity of produce for several families and then have the shares sitting on their front porch or patios for neighbors to pick up. Be creative—distribution can be handled many different ways, depending on the space you have. Work out the way that works best for your members with your facilities.

Fresh picked, local produce ready for pickup at the Enright CSA greenhouse (PHOTO: ERUEV)

SITE CHALLENGES

Now you have found the perfect places to start growing food for your urban CSA, but you aren't quite ready to farm yet. There are a few other things you are going to have to think about—important things like zoning, water availability, and yes, perhaps paying for the use of the land and the water. There are challenges to every undertaking, but if you have the will, there's always a way.

Zoning

Keep zoning in mind when you are looking for land to farm. We have not had an issue with this yet, but there is always a chance that it could become a problem if you ignore it. Even though we have not found any restrictions on using backyards or other city land to grow produce, we have discovered that there are restrictions on composting. In the city of Cincinnati, you can compost in your own yard, but there are strict restrictions on composting on other land.

If you include animals, you may find both zoning and health department issues to consider. For example, in Cincinnati, there are no zoning restrictions on keeping chickens, but you must follow fairly strict health department regulations to keep them in a city yard.

Be aware that laws vary from one jurisdiction to another. Cincinnati has one set of zoning and health laws, nearby unincorporated areas have more or less restrictive regulations, and other municipalities and villages have their own laws. Rules can also vary depending on the type of agricultural operation; for example, different guidelines may apply to a market garden than would govern an urban farm project growing food for a member organization. A CSA usually has less restrictions and applicable laws because food is not being sold directly to the public, but you do need to keep food safety in mind. Chapter 6 has more information about GAP (Good Agricultural Practices) programs and instruction for CSAs.

Soil Testing and Remediation

In an urban area, the land you use to farm may have once been the site of a house or business, or it may simply be too rocky or clay-based for agriculture. In most cases, you will want to have the soil tested for lead and other contamination. In the city of Cincinnati, a program to encourage urban gardening that began in 2009 offered soil testing at little or no cost; you may find a similar program in place, or you can find a lab to test your soil online.

WHAT'S THE BUZZ

The OSU Extension Service provides a fact sheet about soil testing at http://ohioline.osu.edu/hyg-fact/1000/pdf/1132.pdf.

The Hamilton County Soil and Water Conservation District offer a low-price soil fertility kit you can use to test the soil yourself. County residents can pick up soil test kits for $5; if you are a nonresident, you can purchase a soil test kit for $12. More information about the soil test kits is available at Hamilton County Soil and Water Conservation District offices, located at 22 Triangle Park Dr. ,Cincinnati, Ohio; telephone (513) 772-7645; website www.hcswcd.org.

If the soil needs amelioration, your farmer will be able to guide you in what needs to be down to make the land farmable. We have a fairly large-scale compost operation, using all of our agricultural waste as well as leaves collected in the neighborhood, so we create some of our own soil amendment. Although the issue of having safe and arable soil is important, it isn't insurmountable. But do keep in mind that soil testing is a first step when you find the land for your urban farm.

Availability of Water

Land without access to a water source greatly limits what can be grown there and how the food is grown. In our midwestern climate, we go through dry spells almost every summer. There are a few plants that do not require a lot of water, but you cannot build a CSA around such crops. And you can count on nature to take care of the watering through rain most of the time, but you will almost certainly see a time, probably at the height of summer, when you are going to have to water the plants.

If you are farming in neighborhood backyards, you won't have to worry too much about this problem, because almost all homes have a water source. You do need to consider how you will reimburse the home-owner for the water used. The easiest way to calculate this is to take the previous year's water bill(s) from before the backyard was used for CSA farming, and subtract that amount from the bills for water use during the time the CSA is using water for the garden. It may not be exactly accurate, but it will be close enough to assess the basic CSA usage to determine how much to reimburse the homeowner.

Vacant lots and public property can be more challenging when it comes to locating a water source. If the land is in the city and has a municipal water hookup, it is usually possible to install a meter on a faucet. If there isn't water on site, you may be able to get approval to use a metered fire hydrant to water the garden. Or you can try approaching a homeowner close to the garden plot to see if they would allow you to use their water for the garden in exchange for compensation, similar to using water from a member's house to irrigate

A barrel or other container to catch rain water is an economical and sustainable way to provide water for irrigation of garden plots, even when city water is available

a backyard garden. At our new CMHA garden site, we have contracted with nearby homeowners to cover the owners' water bill during the growing season in exchange for using their water.

You can also consider collecting water in rain barrels or other large water containers if there is a building nearby with drainpipes that can be used to fill the containers. However, in this case, the amount of water is limited by how large the containers are—and how often it rains during the growing season. Finally, you can look into the feasibility of carrying water to the site, either manually or with a plastic tank fitted in the back of a pickup truck, but this would likely be a major challenge. We strongly recommend that you not take on land for a garden without first working out the watering issue.

BACK TO THE LAND

If you have willing members with sunny backyards or a community garden that needs someone to take it over, you are well on your way to starting your urban CSA. If neither of these simple solutions is in the cards, however, don't despair. There *is* land in or near your neighborhood available for growing food. You just might need a little help—and some time and perseverance—to find it and work out an arrangement to use it.

Some resources you might be able to use to find help include your local agriculture extension agent. Most counties have agriculture extension programs, and it's worth a call to see if someone has been down the same path before and the agent can give you some ideas on where urban farming has taken root in your community in the past.

A Farmer's Guide to Securing Land, published by California FarmLink in 2008, provides tools and examples to help keep farmland in viable agriculture. It is geared more toward traditional rural farming, but it also describes several different land tenure "models" including leases, partnerships, and ownership, which might be helpful if you are looking to lease or buy property.

DIG DEEPER

A Farmers' Guide to Securing Land is available online at http:// www.californiafarmlink.org.

The USDA Farm Service Agency (FSA) has two programs for land purchase that specifically benefit beginning and socially disadvantaged farmers. If your urban CSA is in an inner city neighborhood with a high poverty rate, it may qualify for the Direct Farm Ownership Loan Program.

You are thinking about starting a co-operative urban CSA—a challenging concept in itself. You are going to have to think creatively to solve many problems that arise. Finding suitable land and negotiating a way to use it is step one—so start thinking "outside the box," and you'll discover that possible sites are abundant. As a bonus, the connections you make when you talk to landowners, school principals, recreation center managers, and other people in the community while looking for land may be invaluable when you reach other steps in the process of organizing your CSA. ◾

Chapter 3

Finding People to Join Your CSA

I hope some day you'll join us,
And the world will be as one.
—John Lennon

You've found land to farm in your urban neighborhood, and now you need to find other people to join you in the work of growing food locally—and enjoying the produce you'll harvest. The time is right. The local food movement is growing quickly and people are enthusiastic about growing their own food.

The enthusiasm of your core group is the best place to start when it comes to recruiting members. You all know people who are interested in local food—or being more self-sustaining—helping the environment—or simply improving the neighborhood. After you get a few more enthusiastic people involved, things will start moving, as those people tell even more people about the new venture.

MEMBER RECRUITMENT

Set a specific number of shares you know you can handle the first year. Don't grow too big too fast; starting small and growing gradually will allow you to iron out the wrinkles in the CSA setup as you go. Also, take the time to get your membership information organized before

Let people know what they can expect to receive in a weekly CSA share and you'll find your produce speaks for itself (Photo: ERUEV)

you start recruiting seriously. It's great to get a few people on board early, especially if they are people who will be involved in the planning and organization of the CSA, but get a few simple marketing tools together early on so you can answer questions from prospective members sensibly and completely.

Start with a simple brochure that explains what you are doing, gives the location, share sizes and prices, and contact information to find out more. You definitely need a phone number that someone will answer—or return messages from—and a simple way for people to contact you online. At first that may be an email address, and maybe a Facebook page or a page on a community website, but eventually you may want to create a website for the CSA that you can direct prospects to so they can get more information. But first you need to find enough people to make your CSA successful and self-sustaining, and the best way to do it is by word of mouth.

What Motivates People to Join a CSA?

You need to know where to look for people and know what to offer them to make them want to join. So you need to think about the motivating factors that will convince people that membership in an urban CSA is for them.

The first step is thinking about why you are interested in urban farming:

▶ *To eat better.* This can mean healthier eating, but it also can mean having food that tastes better because it is fresher. You'll try new foods and will find some that you like a lot.

▶ *To become part of the local food movement.* People are tired of having only a few choices in varieties of common produce—Iceberg or leaf lettuce? Red Delicious apples or Granny Smiths? A CSA can introduce people to different varieties of familiar food, too.

▶ *To avoid processed and genetically modified food.* Much food that travels long distances is highly processed using preservatives to keep it stable until it is sold. And we've all read stories about experiments with "Frankenfood" involving genetic modification to produce longer-lasting, less perishable produce. This kind of long-distance food gives up a lot of taste to make it transportable (just think of a cottony tasting tomato bought at a supermarket in January), and you may not want all those chemicals in your food.

▶ *To help the environment.* If a lot of food is grown in your own neighborhood, you will immediately reduce your carbon footprint substantially. It's estimated that the average American meal "travels" 1500 miles to get to your plate. Locally grown food doesn't require so much fossil fuel use, and less fossil fuel also means less CO_2 emissions.

DIG DEEPER

How far does your food travel before you eat it? Find out more about the loneliness of the long-distance produce at http://www.cuesa.org/page/how-far-does-your-food-travel-get-your-plate.

Research indicates that most people who join a CSA think that their eating habits will change drastically, and they are ready and willing to accept that change. That kind of thinking may be unrealistic, however. People get set in their ways, and changing in a major way—having someone else, essentially, decide most of what you are going to eat for five or six months a year—is a big commitment.

Many people quickly become accustomed to picking up their weekly share and discovering new kinds of produce, new varieties of vegetables, however. They find recipes that they love and they can't wait until kale—or bok choi or daikon—is in the share again. They tell friends and family about how great it is to eat local, seasonal, tasty, and healthy food that they have helped grow.

WHAT'S THE BUZZ

Direct potential members to a short film, "Community Supported Agriculture: What to Expect When You Join a Farm," available on YouTube. Although it is geared more toward joining a traditional, farmer-owned rural CSA, it will give people an idea of what is involved.

But there are always exceptions. Some statistics indicate that a CSA is likely to lose 10 to 40 percent of their members at the end of the season. For some, learning how to cook new things is just too much work. When it's high harvest time and shares are rolling in produce, it can be overwhelming to figure out what to do with ten cucumbers or a dozen squash.

There are other reasons why people leaving a CSA. Some move away, have increased demands on their lives, or feel as if they live too far from the CSA to participate fully. Other people may find that they don't actually cook as much as they thought or hoped they would, and some may not have expected to get so many unfamiliar foods. It's important to offer the right balance of familiar items and new or unusual produce to keep people who need a little encouragement to move outside their comfort zone when it comes to eating. In most organizations, one should anticipate a 30% loss of membership per year, and a CSA is no exception to this rule of thumb.

How to Find People to Participate

There are a lot of ways to recruit new members. Remember, you are a local urban farm project, so most of your members will come from nearby. Get the word out in your community. Encourage new members to tell their friends about the CSA. You might even consider having a promotion, such as 5% off the cost of a share or five free work hours for every new member whom an established member brings into the group.

There are plenty of other ways to let people know about the new urban farm, too:

▶ Talk to someone at the local paper about writing an article on what you are doing. The article may not appear in print, but most newspapers have a website for local stories, and you can direct people to the article online.

▶ Get that brochure put together, print some copies at the local print shop on a brightly colored paper, and distribute them wherever you can—schools, libraries, churches, community groups, bus stops, and if you can, on the bulletin board of your local supermarket.

▶ If people ask you about the CSA, give them two brochures—an extra one for a friend.

▶ Get listed on the locavore websites in your area. In Cincinnati, the Central Ohio River Valley (CORV) food guide lists local farms and CSAs in an annual directory; they also have a website with the information. Make sure you are in any directory like this you can find.

▶ Give presentations to civic groups and community organizations to let people know about your urban farm. Your community council, Kiwanis club, or other organization will be happy to give you 15 minutes or a half hour to tell their group about what you are doing because what you are doing is going to help the community. Put together a simple PowerPoint if you can, or make a display board to bring along, and take those brochures with you, too.

▶ Talk to a local radio show or your community access cable television show about coming on as a guest to talk to the show's host about what you are doing. Be sure to have an email address, telephone number, or simple website address you can give out for more information.

ENRIGHT RIDGE
COMMUNITY SUPPORTED AGRICULTURE
LOCALLY GROWN PRODUCE MAY THROUGH NOVEMBER!

Join the only urban CSA in Cincinnati

Work to grow your own produce

Become a locavore this summer

Details and application at

www.enright-csa.org

Find us on Facebook

A simple flyer or brochure you can distribute around your neighborhood can direct potential members to find current information about your CSA online

▶ Visit any businesses that have offices in your area and ask to put brochures in their common room, put a notice in their company newsletter, or hang a sign on their bulletin board. People who work in the neighborhood can get involved through their workplace.

▶ Have brochures with you when you go to a local farmer's market or even out to eat at a neighborhood restaurant. Ask if you can leave a few brochures on the front counter at the restaurant and pass one on to anyone you strike up a conversation with at the farmer's market.

SETTING SHARE SIZES AND PRICES

You have to give people an idea of how much produce they are going to receive, and you need to set a price for the share. Members are going to want value for their contributions (both monetary and work hours), but you also want to be careful that you don't overwhelm them with too much food. If half the share winds up on the compost pile at a member's house every week, it's not the right size.

Determining Share Size

Things to consider when you are determining share size include:

▶ How long is the growing season? How many weeks of the year will people receive a share?

▶ Do you have a greenhouse or hoop house to start crops early and to allow for succession planting in the same beds?

▶ What kind of storage area do you have for things that can be stored for awhile after they are harvested (onions, potatoes, and garlic, for example)?

▶ Do you have cold storage for more perishable produce?

▶ Do you want to have one standard size, or does it make more sense to offer two or three different sizes to attract families as well as couples or single people?

▶ How will you handle members who "share a share"?

At Enright CSA, we have offered two different size shares, which we have called by various names. At first we had full and half shares, then we changed the names to large and regular shares. In both cases, the larger one fed four (4) or more people a week and the smaller size provided enough produce for two or three (2–3) people a week. And we encourage people to find other folks to share a share, if that is what works for them. But we have learned that it's best to make the members responsible for the logistics of sharing—they decide how to divide the cost and work hours among themselves, and most important, they either come together to pick up their produce, or one person picks up the entire share and distributes produce to the other members. It just doesn't work to have various people show up to get their part of a share when it might include one pumpkin or a handful of basil, things that can't be divided very well.

CSAs generally provide produce—vegetables, greens, sometimes fruits or nuts. But many CSAs also offer other items in shares, including eggs, dairy, meat, bread, honey, and even flowers. Offering these kinds of items can add another level of complexity to the CSA operation, so we recommend you start with produce and then decide how you want to grow and expand in succeeding seasons.

Setting a Price

How do you determine the price for a share in your urban CSA? It's difficult to do because there are so many variables. But consider some advice from the University of California Cooperative Extension: Setting the share price too low is "the biggest contributing factor to CSA burnout and failure." On the other hand, you know your community and have a good idea of what the market will bear. You don't want to price yourself out of contention, either.

The best place to start is with your budget. Determine likely expenses, including seeds, equipment, staff salaries (at least a farmer, and possibly assistant farmers and a farm manager or CSA coordinator), land costs, water costs, and other expenses. It's important to include all the costs involved. This includes fair wages for labor as well as hidden or indirect expenses such as insurance, repairs and maintenance, capital improvements, and taxes, if applicable.

Then, take the total amount and divide it by the number of shares you expect to have for the CSA. That will give you

WHAT'S THE BUZZ

A simple equation for figuring out what to set as the price for a CSA share:

EXPENSES / NUMBER OF SHARES = SHARE PRICE

the per-share price. If you are going to have different levels of membership, use a method to determine the prices for different size shares that makes sense. Try to keep it simple for figuring prices.

County extension offices may be able to provide budget examples that will help you itemize all the costs of urban farming, and there is a sample CSA budget in Appendix A, p. 102. You should also look at comparable CSA farms in your region to see what they charge for a share. In southwest Ohio, the CORV Food Guide (*http://www.eatlocalcorv.org/*) lists information about CSA share prices, and you can find listings for other regions online.

As a general estimate, current CSA shares in the Midwest range from about $300 to $700 per share for a season, depending on the location, the type of CSA, and the size of the share. It's important to make sure shareholders pay enough to cover all the costs of the food they receive, and it is equally important that they believe they are getting a good value in belonging to a CSA. Finding the balance there—and also considering intangibles such as "goodwill," the knowledge that members are supporting local and environmentally sustainable food production and contributing to the health of their community in many ways—will help you determine the cost of a share.

When you evaluate the share price for your CSA, use these criteria:

▶ You are happy with the price you have set.

▶ Members are happy with the price and the size of the share they receive.

▶ You have met your membership goal for the season; that is, you have sold all your shares.

▶ Your costs have been covered.

▶ Your farmer and paid staff members have received a fair wage for their labor.

If you have met all (or most) of these criteria, your share cost is appropriate. Of course, even if you have met these criteria one season, changing prices and markets will demand you re-evaluate share prices before the beginning of each succeeding season.

CO-OP HOURS, ALL-WORK SHARES, AND NONWORK SHARES

A co-op urban farm project keeps the costs associated with farming lower by depending on volunteer hours from shareholders to take care of many tasks involved with running the CSA. This involves another kind of bookkeeping—figuring out how many hours of work are required for each share. Some cooperative CSAs are run by the farmer, who coordinates members with work shares to do much of the administrative work.

At the Enright Ridge CSA, most of our members work a set number of hours in addition to paying for their share. Currently we require 40 hours of work over the course of the 26-week season (with some work hours available pre-and post-season) for a full share, and 20 hours of work for a half share. Shareholders keep track of the hours they work on preprinted forms (in Appendix A, p. 103) that we keep in a binder at the greenhouse. Work is divided into teams, and team leaders let people know when there are tasks to be done.

We have work directly related to farming—everything from making soil mixes and transplanting young plants to watering, weeding, bed preparation, and harvesting. We have a compost team that works all year round to provide us with soil amendment for our gar-

There is work for everyone on the urban farm, including keeping up with turning the compost piles (PHOTO: NANCY SULLIVAN)

dens, and during growing season we have a whole team set up to handle distribution of shares on Saturday mornings.

We also need people to do a lot of work associated with running the business side of the CSA, such as accounting, communications, fundraising, and grant writing, and we have people who organize social events and who know about plumbing, carpentry, and glazing, to help maintain our greenhouse.

There's work for everybody, but not everybody works. We have some nonwork shares, which cost more. We encourage people to work—there are even a few "all-work" shares that require more than 100 hours of labor—but we understand that there are people who prefer to pay instead of work. We're happy to welcome them, too, though we limit both the number of nonwork shares and all-work shares.

It may seem like a difficult task to juggle all these different kinds of work shares, but so far it has been manageable for us. We have come up with a pretty good system—we set the price of a work hour at $5. Therefore, if you want a nonwork share for a share size that normally requires 40 hours of work, you'll be paying an extra $200 for your share. So far, this has worked for us.

We've also used this system when people do not fulfill their work hours. Most people do, and many work more than their allotted hours, but sometimes members wind up a little short on hours. They are billed for hours not worked at $5 per hour, and the CSA gets some extra income at the end of the season.

The thing to remember is that every farm and every CSA is different. These are guidelines you can use when setting your share price and work hours, but you will have to tailor your price and work requirements to *your* CSA and *your* members.

> ### WHAT'S THE BUZZ
>
> You may find that you want to set the "hourly wage" that you use to calculate nonwork shares and hours owed at a higher rate than $5. Keep in mind "what the traffic will bear" in your community when setting share prices and calculating the worth of volunteer hours. It's a balancing act; you don't want to undervalue the work of members, nor make the nonwork prohibitively expensive.

RETAINING MEMBERS

You will have to resign yourself to the fact that some members come and go, staying only a season or two, but you want to make sure that most of your members keep coming back year after year. Every aspect of an urban CSA affects member retention—problems with share produce, work hours, other members or the staff—all these things can mean the difference between someone staying for another season or calling it quits.

Of course, there are other reasons why people leave. People move, they start their own gardens (or their own CSAs!), or they just rethink their priorities. They may have thought they were going to spend evenings cooking delicious meals of home-grown produce and weekends freezing and canning the extra vegetables, but when they find that the produce is turning brown before they can get to it, they start to think twice about belonging to the CSA.

Losing 10 to 20% of your membership each year is not unusual. If you find that your turnover is closer to 50%, try to find out what is causing so many people to leave. It doesn't hurt to ask people who aren't coming back why they've decided not to return; maybe you can even convince some of those folks to stay if they know something is going to change.

One good way to retain members is to ask at the end of one season for a commitment for the following season. You can offer a discounted rate for early deposits to encourage people to sign up.

Stay Connected

Stay connected with your members. A CSA is a co-operative venture, and when people come back year after year, it is because they feel they are a part of something special—they have made a connection to the CSA. Make members feel appreciated, and make it as easy as possible for them to stay involved. Make sure they know about work opportunities and social events, and find out what they like and don't like about how the CSA is run. You can do this with a member surveys that asks what the CSA is doing right—and what can be improved.

END-OF-SEASON SURVEYS

At the end of each season, we've distributed surveys to our members and asked them questions that help us get an idea of how the CSA is succeeding. Ask members about:

▶ The produce they liked best, and what they liked least

▶ If their expectations were met, and if not, how they were not met

▶ The most enjoyable tasks at the CSA, and the tasks they liked least

▶ How the pickup/distribution of shares worked for them

▶ If they got enough—and not too much—communication from the CSA about what was going on

▶ Whether or not they liked the social events associated with the farm

▶ What else they'd like to see at the CSA—other products or events or a different way of doing things

▶ Any additional comments they might have about the season just past

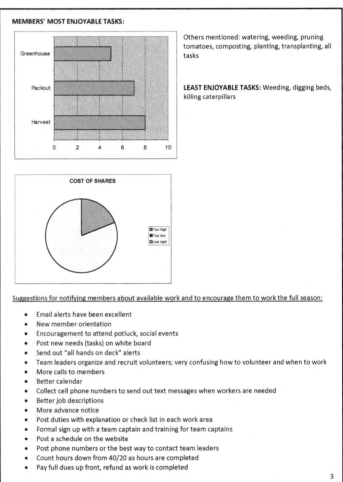

Results of a survey of CSA members to find out what they liked about the season and what they think could be improved

Here are a few other suggestions we've gleaned from looking at other people's surveys. First, keep it short. People are busy, and they aren't going to want to spend a lot of time on this. Ask the least number of questions you can to reasonably get the information you need, and make it easy and quick for members to respond.

Provide a range when possible. That is, instead of Yes/No responses to questions about what they thought of the variety, amount, cost, and other variables at your CSA, ask them to rate the particular issue on a scale of 1 to 5. This can give you some good information. Be sure to provide guidance for the scale—that is, label it clearly with "Agree" and "Disagree" or "Satisfied" and "Dissatisfied" or even "Excellent" and "Poor" to indicate what the ends of the scale mean.

And finally, keep it relevant. Ask for members' attitudes about things that can change. If you can't grow fruit, don't ask people what kind of fruit they'd like to see in the share. On the other hand, if you are thinking about changing pickup locations, ask members what locations would be most satisfying to them. You want information about things you *can* change and ways you *can* do better. Don't disappoint people by asking them about things you can't change.

DIG DEEPER

You can access the complete results of the Enright Ridge CSA survey by clicking *Enright CSA Survey Results* at http:// www.enright-csa.org/newsletter.html.

We have gotten a decent response to the surveys we distribute—almost all of our members took a paper copy of the survey or printed a copy from a link sent by email, and 70 percent of the surveys were returned. Volunteers tabulate the survey answers to make the information useful to the membership as a whole as well as to the core committee as they steer the CSA toward a new season. We published the results as a short document that is accessible from the News page of our website.

MARKETING YOUR CSA

If you have members who have some experience in marketing, ask them to think about ways to get the word out about the CSA to attract new members and retain the members you have. This is an especially good job for the off season, when you are not busy growing vegetables.

Doing a little marketing in the off season has a twofold benefit—first, you may encourage people to look you up and join the CSA. You also may find that getting the word out about your urban CSA inspires other groups to try urban farming. It never hurts to get a little good publicity.

If your community has a weekly paper, send them a prewritten article (with a photograph) about your farm project, and there's a good chance they'll publish it. Most community papers depend on readers for a lot of their content these days. The daily paper in your city or town—or a local radio or television station—may also be interested in publishing an article about your CSA, perhaps in a special green living section or at the right time of year, when gardens are "in the news," usually at planting time in the spring or traditional harvest time in the fall.

We've found that alternative press outlets, such as weekly arts papers and magazines devoted to topics such as urban living or culinary pursuits, have shown an interest in what we are doing. We've had nice articles in several of these magazines, and one article leads to another. That's true about all publicity—the more you get, the more interest there is.

Not too long ago, we were approached by the Cincinnati Contemporary Art Center to be a part of an art project that involved having an artist build a custom-made bike cart for our CSA. Not only did we get a great tool for our gardens, but we also garnered quite a lot of publicity when the bike cart was finished and delivered. Then, it became part of an exhibit on art and farming at the museum, and that reaped even more publicity.

We've also participated in conferences, tastings, seminars, and classes that gather people who are working on various kinds of agricultural projects and urban and community farming in particular, networking and making connections that have helped our CSA grow. Cincinnati's Civic Garden Center, for example, has a "Taste of Local Gardens" event every September, where urban farms share what they've grown.

This bike cart, used to haul tools to the garden plots and produce back to the greenhouse, was custom built for the Enright CSA by a Danish artist, through the Cincinnati Contemporary Arts Center, which sponsored an exhibit of art on the farm, and the bike cart and exhibit both got some publicity for our urban farm project

A FEW FINAL THOUGHTS

You want to find and keep people involved in your CSA. One way to help people feel welcome is to ask established members to pair with new members so each one has one person they can ask about problems or concerns and who can introduce them to staff, team leaders, and other members. Having someone you know to go with you will encourage new members to attend work sessions and social events, too.

Finally, consistently meeting member expectations is the best way to keep them coming back. If there is always plenty of variety and your produce is high quality, make sure it stays that way. Keep your pickup time and place consistent, and set work schedules and keep to them. Have regularly scheduled events and let people know about them in advance. With a CSA, the less surprises, the better—give your members what they want and they'll keep coming back. ■

Chapter 4

The Business Side: Managing and Financing Your CSA

*When you concentrate on agriculture
and are frugal in expenditures,
Heaven cannot impoverish your state.*

—Xun Zi

Remember that your urban farm is a business, and you must consider this aspect of urban farming as you plan your startup. The two main things to consider on the business side of a CSA are what kind of management or administrative structure you will use and how you will finance the endeavor, and those are the subjects of this chapter. We will also cover some basic insurance considerations and end with a few thoughts about how to make a difference in our economy—or create a new kind of economy.

THE ADMINISTRATIVE STRUCTURE

We began the Enright Ridge CSA in November 2008, bringing together a dozen people interested in setting up an urban farm project. One of the people in the group was an experienced farmer who became our CSA's first lead farmer. We are aware that having the farmer on board as part of the organization from the beginning gave us a big head start in getting the farm operational by spring 2009.

Some of the initial issues the organizing committee had to deal with included finding the land, recruiting shareholders, developing a budget, working out the finances, establishing how the CSA would collect money and track work hours from members, and keeping records.

Our CSA began as a project of the nonprofit Enright Ridge Urban EcoVillage (ERUEV), an established entity in Price Hill that is working towards sustainable living in a city neighborhood. Our association with a nonprofit from the start has given us several advantages:

- ▶ We were able to apply for grants for the CSA (which we used to purchase a greenhouse).

- ▶ We applied for and were allocated several AmeriCorps volunteers in the first three seasons.

- ▶ We had access to a bookkeeping system already in place.

However, the relationship also created another layer of administration. Since we are part of ERUEV, we must receive approval from its board for some of our actions, especially those that relate to finances. Several original CSA shareholders were members of the ERUEV board, which assisted us in working with it.

In developing a structure for your CSA, it is important to work with the assets that you have. You may have land, a farmer, potential members, a small group of people who are highly committed to the CSA's success, start-up funds, or some mix of these. Consider the assets you have and make the most of them; they are the building blocks you need to plan around and use as the foundation for your CSA.

Management/Directors

We developed what we called a "core group," a small committee of people who wanted to see the project succeed. They took on the management of the farm project. We were also fortunate enough to be able to participate in the AmeriCorps program, which matches people willing to work for low wages—volunteers who earn a small stipend, essentially—with positions that make an impact in city neighborhoods.

This made it possible for us to hire one of the core group members as a half-time administrator for the CSA in its initial season, which was a great help in starting out. However, in subsequent seasons we ran the CSA with a strongly committed volunteer administrator, and that model was also successful. In our fourth season, we made plans to hire a part-time administrator to handle management tasks. We've discovered that there is a definite need for one or two people to handle the administrative tasks of the CSA, but the structure for this position can be set up in more than one way.

WHAT'S THE BUZZ

One of the advantages of a nonprofit organization is the ability to write and receive grants to help fund some aspects of the urban CSA.

The important thing is to have a system in place to handle the day-to-day business of the CSA that is not directly related to farming. This gives the farmer the time to plan and do the farming. That said, there are many traditional, farmer-owned CSAs that are run and managed by the farmer alone or with help from family members. We have found, however, that it makes sense to have someone other than the farmer to manage the work not directly associated with farming. The important thing to remember is that there's more to the CSA than just growing food, and it's all those other things that need administrative oversight.

Structuring the Business of the CSA

Our CSA is a co-operative. We hire and pay a farmer to manage the crops and arrange for an administrator and team leaders to take care of the many other tasks, from watering plants to making compost to sending out a newsletter. This book is concerned with how you can best accomplish urban farming, and whereas being part of a nonprofit organization and functioning as a co-op has worked for us, there are other structures or models that you might find will serve you better, such as one of the following.

Sole Proprietorship. Most small farms are organized as a sole proprietorship. An individual owns the farm, the farmer is responsible for all debts and obligations, and he also takes all profits. Pros: This type of farm business is easy to start; one person makes all the decisions; taxes are levied according to the farmer's personal income. Cons: It can be difficult to borrow money for this type of business; it is cumbersome to transfer the farm to heirs.

General Partnership. Two or more people invest in and share in management of the business. Partners share debts and obligations; responsibilities are typically spelled out in a partnership agreement. Pros: Partnership is fairly easy to organize; initial costs are low; the partnership can own assets and enter into contracts; partners provide a larger pool of resources than an individual. Cons: Each partner is liable for all obligations and may be held liable for obligations of another partner; control is shared, so having a wrong partner can be a major disaster, and if one partner wants to leave, the farm must be reorganized.

Limited Partnership. The limited partnership is a formal agreement between one or more general partners and one or more limited partners. Limited partners are primarily a source of capital and have no voice in management. Profits are divided among the investors. Pros: Each limited partner is liable for debts only up to the amount of his/her investment in the company; limited partner interests can be sold to raise capital. Cons: It can be costly to set up a limited partnership; accounting and state reporting requirements can be onerous; at least one general partner must be fully liable for partnership obligations.

> **WHAT'S THE BUZZ**
>
> The **Family Limited Partnership** is a special form of limited partnership in most states.

Corporation. The corporation is the most complex business structure that would typically be considered by an agricultural business. It is the structure of most large agri-businesses. The corporation is a separate legal entity comprised of shareholders, directors, and officers. A corporation can enter into contracts, own property, and act as a separate legal entity. Pros: No shareholder, officer, or director can be held liable for debts unless a law is broken; interest in the business can be readily sold. Cons: This structure can lead to a lack of personal responsibility and commitment to the farm; startup costs can be high; articles of incorporation and extensive record keeping and filing of reports are required.

Limited Liability Company (LLC). A limited liability company is a business entity that combines the limited liability of a corporation with the flexible management options of a general partnership. Pros: Can be organized as a partnership but without the liability burden of a general partnership. Cons: The setup for an LLC can be complicated and expensive setup; there are complex accounting and reporting requirements; ownership of an LLC does not transfer easily.

If you are interested in any of these business models for your CSA, you will need to find out more and get legal advice about how to proceed.

Finding Qualified Farmers

Some farms begin with a farmer. If you are contemplating starting an urban CSA because your group includes an experienced farmer, you are one step ahead of the game. The most important person in your organization is already there.

If you have the vision for a CSA but you don't have a farmer, start the search process by doing a little planning first. Work out how you plan to compensate the farmer. Compensation can include a salary, of course, but there are also less tangible forms of compensation including health insurance, workers' compensation coverage, a share of the food, lodging, and of course, the opportunity to farm—all of which may be provided to the farmer in the way of payment for his/her services. The farmer can be paid a salary as an employee of the CSA or may be hired as a contractor. You will set these terms or negotiate with the farmer during the hiring process. As a startup with members working alongside the farmer, you may find that a part-time farmer may be sufficient to meet the needs of your CSA. Our lead farmer was half time for the first four years of our operation.

If there is no farmer already involved in your organization, start your search locally. Begin by networking with food groups in the area. In Cincinnati, the

The most important factor in your CSA is the farmer—you need a competent farmer to oversee the growing process (PHOTO: NANCY SULLIVAN)

Central Ohio River Valley (CORV) local food directory has a list of local CSAs, farms, and food groups; people involved with these organizations may know about farmers in the area who are looking for positions or may be able to publicize your need for a farmer. If you can't find a farmer locally, look at these same types of groups in nearby cities. There are also national groups interested in quality local food and farms that may be able to help you find a farmer.

When you have found a few likely candidates, interview them carefully. Develop your interview questions in advance and make sure they relate to the candidate's experience and the CSA's needs. Ask for references—and be sure to check them! You'll want to find someone with the right qualifications, but keep in mind your farmer will also need to have the right personality and motivation to fit in with your group and the vision you have for your urban CSA.

It's a good idea to have more than one candidate during the interview process. It's also a good idea to have more than one person involved in meeting and interviewing the candidates. Getting input from several people on a hiring committee can make you look at all aspects of a candidate's qualifications and will enable you to make a better decision. Take advantage of technology, setting up a conference call, for example, to efficiently screen candidates before setting up formal interviews. We were able to do our first interview with candidates from out of town using Skype, which saved time and resources for us and for the potential farmers.

DIG DEEPER

Some of the interview questions developed by Enright CSA in the farmer search process are included on pp. 104–105 in Appendix A of this manual.

Training Staff

Of course it's best to hire a farmer with CSA experience, but even an experienced farmer needs to keep learning. There are new ideas and practices that can help make your farm more productive and more sustainable. The Ohio Ecological Food and Farm Association (OEFFA) is one source of information, and they sponsor an annual conference every February. They also have local chapters in Cincinnati and other parts of the state. If you are thinking of start-ing a CSA in Ohio, join OEFFA and attend local chapter meetings and the annual conference; you'll learn a lot from people with experience.

DIG DEEPER

Join the Ohio Ecological Food and Farm Association at http://www.oeffa.org.

We also encourage your CSA and your farmer to develop a training program for assistant farmers or interns. Urban farming is a growing area and you will find there are people who want to learn how to grow food locally and sustainably in your area. Providing both didactic instruction and on-the-job training will make the experi-ence more valuable to your interns and farm assistants, and providing a good training program will draw people to your CSA.

Sharing information with other CSAs about how to succeed, especially in urban farming, is another way to support the movement to local food, and your farmer may gain valuable information by making these connections.

Encourage your farmer to initiate a training program for assistant farmers or interns to train more people who want to learn how to grow food locally and sustainably in urban neighborhoods (PHOTO: NANCY SULLIVAN)

Training and Encouraging Volunteers

You will probably find you have two kinds of volunteers at your CSA. There are those for whom coming to work at the farm is a one-time event; these may be students or others looking for community service hours or people who just want to find out what you are doing. You may have other volunteers who don't want to become shareholders, but want to volunteer with your farm. Then there are your shareholder members, who sign up to provide a set number of work hours to the co-op farm operation.

We have high school students who come to work on Saturday mornings, with different students each session. For these groups, we provide an introduction about what we do and why we are doing it, and we help them see how the work they will be doing fits into the effort. Then we show them how to do the work and they set to the tasks.

Students from a nearby high school complete service hours and learn about urban farming on Saturday mornings

For ongoing volunteers and for your shareholder members who will be working at the CSA regularly, it is important to find out what they hope to gain from the experience. When people (volunteers) are matched with work that suits them and that they can competently fulfill, the whole group will benefit. Make sure that the extent of work required is clearly spelled out in the application for volunteers and the application to become a CSA member. On the other hand, you don't want to discourage anyone. We have members in our CSA of all ages; some people are young enough to be able to do sometimes backbreaking work preparing beds or harvesting vegetables; others are more suited to lighter jobs such as watering in the greenhouse or mixing soil. Still others can handle administrative or organizational tasks. There is a job for everyone.

You can't always meet the needs of a volunteer, however, and sometimes other commitments will keep a volunteer or co-op member from being able to complete their work hours. It's a good idea to have a contract with ongoing volunteers and members that spells out their responsibilities and commitment to the CSA and the CSA's commitment to them. In our culture, volunteerism is not always held in high esteem, and people sometimes think if it is inconvenient to work at a time they have agreed to, it won't matter if they don't show up. If they can't do it, then they need to let you know—or they may not be a good fit for your CSA.

Working with Work Shares

Some CSAs do not have work shares. They are operated by a farmer or a group who grows the food and distributes it to their members. This is a structure that works well, especially if the CSA is small. However, the co-operative model for urban farming, with members who sign up for shares that have both a monetary cost and a work commitment, is a great way to accomplish the work that needs to be done as well as a way to develop community and commitment.

Our CSA allows people to choose a work share or a nonwork share. The commitment involved in our work shares has ranged from 10 hours to 40 hours, with most of the work hours scheduled during our six-month growing season. This structure has provided us with a large pool of workers, and most of our work

Starting Your Urban CSA

share members take their commitment seriously. Every year some members work more hours than required. We have also had a few people who did not meet their work requirement, but in these instances, the member has almost always been willing to make up the difference financially.

The biggest struggle we have found with work shares is having people available to work when and where they are needed. We have experimented with a number of different structures and have found that the most effective system is to set up teams with a strong team leader who is willing to communicate with team members about when and where work needs to be done. Our teams include:

1. Core Committee (or core group), the administrative and planning group for the CSA

2. Membership, recruiting and retaining members

3. Communications, handling electronic and traditional ways of disseminating information

4. Land Development, researching places we can use to farm

5. Resources, overseeing finances and fundraising

6. Nursery Care, propagating seeds and seedlings

7. Irrigation, watering the crops

8. Harvest, bringing in the crops from the fields and gardens

9. Packout, handling distribution of produce

10. Social, setting up meetings, potlucks, and other get-togethers

11. Marketing, letting people know about what we are doing

In addition to these, last year we also tried setting up teams for each of the different garden areas or combination of plots. In past seasons, we had a Soil/Bed Preparation team, a Transplant team, a Crop Care and Culture team, and a Pest Management team, but having teams that handle all of these tasks for one garden has proved more efficient for us. This year it has been decided to have just one production team to do all of these tasks. Finding the right combination of teams to organize the work efficiently is an ongoing challenge.

Scheduling work is one of the most difficult tasks. Each team leader helps with scheduling and recruiting members and works to make sure people show up when and where they are needed. A strong team leader can make the difference in the team's success. We have used email notifications and even a Twitter feed to announce work opportunities, and we are now exploring a computerized system for organizing work schedules and sending out information to let members know when and where help is needed.

HANDLING THE CSA'S FINANCES

Funding Startup Costs

In the Enright Ridge CSA, we have a resource committee rather than a finance committee. This is because we don't deal strictly with money—many of the tangible things that we needed to start the urban farm project were provided to us by members and others interested in helping us. It's an economic model that we encourage. You don't have to buy everything new—sometimes you can find just what you need sitting in someone's basement or garage gathering dust.

We needed to pay for some materials such as office supplies and copies as we were starting our CSA. These incidental costs were covered by the people committed to setting up the CSA. Other items could be donated, such as the use of personal phones, a place to meet, even land to start farming and basic garden tools. During our first year, most of the tools we used—including a rototiller—were donated. We also used a greenhouse at a member's house to start plants the first year. We're not saying you can do this with no upfront money at all, but we do suggest that you think creatively about what you need and where you can get it. The Enright CSA has a bicycle-operated cart that we use for carrying tools from the greenhouse to our gardens; it was designed and built for us at no cost as part of an art project at a downtown museum. You never know where you might get a donation of something you can use!

Be creative when it comes finding tools for farming; for example, you can rent larger equipment when you need it, or ask members to donate tools they don't use

When we used land that belonged to members of the fledgling CSA, we offered people a choice of either having a share of the produce with no work hours required or with no fee. A few people accepted this offer, but many simply donated their land, and in some cases they even provided the water to irrigate the gardens we began in their yards. When paying members began signing up, we had income that made it possible for us to begin to pay the farmer and purchase seeds and other materials.

Sponsorships and Grants

You might be able to find sponsors who are willing to provide startup funds for an urban farm project. Ask businesses and individuals in your community who are interested in seeing the CSA prosper in their neighborhood. Grants are also a real possibility if your CSA is set up as a nonprofit organization. If not, you may be able to work with a nonprofit in your neighborhood, such as a community development corporation or a civic group, who want the CSA to succeed and can apply for a grant to aid the startup. We were able to get grants that helped us purchase a greenhouse, tools, and other materials the first year we were in operation.

The Annual Budget

Set an annual budget with expenses equal to or less than expected income. The core group or a budget committee needs to determine expenses. How much will you need to pay the farmer and other staff, take care of any rent, pay water and electric bills if you have a greenhouse or other structure, purchase seeds and other materials, and buy or lease equipment? What other expenses may come up?

The budget also must determine projected income—the amount of money you will bring in from paid shares in the CSA. You may have other sources of income as well, such as grants, donations, or sales at a farmers' market.

Of course, there are variations on the balanced budget. Some co-ops work out a plan that pays the farmer with what is left in income after expenses at the end of the year. Or you may find a magnanimous resident who wants to see the CSA get off the ground and will agree to cover any extra

DIG DEEPER

See Appendix A, p. 102, for an example of an annual budget for a CSA.

costs at the end of the season. One of these alternatives may work for you, but in the end, your outlay and income has to balance, so making a realistic budget and staying within it remains important.

INSURANCE AND LIABILITY ISSUES

You will almost certainly need to consider getting some insurance coverage for your farm project. There are three kinds of insurance that you will hear about when trying to figure out what you need: property insurance, general liability insurance, and crop insurance.

You may also need to provide health insurance for your farmer (see the section earlier in the chapter titled "Finding Qualified Farmers" for more about employment benefits for farmers). If you are going to provide health insurance, look around for the best deal. Ohio Farmers' Union has health insurance for farmers. Our present farmer has health insurance through her spouse, so we have been spared this expense.

Property insurance covers tools, equipment, and other things the CSA owns, including actual property or structures like a greenhouse or garden shed. It's good to have property insurance, because if your greenhouse is damaged in a hailstorm or someone steals your tractor, you will receive compensation.

But liability insurance is probably more important, because it protects you if you are sued by someone (a member or even a trespasser) who is injured in your gardens. If you garden in other people's backyards, it is likely (though not certain) that their homeowners' liability insurance would cover a problem like this, but that doesn't mean the gardens' owners are going to like taking the risk of having to use their insurance to cover a farm-related incident, so you probably want to look into getting your own coverage. If you are associated with a nonprofit organization in your community, you may be able to get liability coverage for the CSA under that organization's existing insurance plans.

If you farm on public property in a community garden or on city-owned lots, you might not need your own insurance plan. Check to see if the property is self-insured by the municipality or township that has jurisdiction over it. In some cases, however, public property used for a community garden requires separate liability insurance plan because it is not be covered by the city. Find out what the situation is with your plots. Garden insurance is a relatively new thing, and some

DIG DEEPER

The American Community Garden Association (ACGA) offers information about garden insurance at http://communitygarden.org/docs/learn/articles/insuranceforcommunitygardens.pdf.

insurance agents may not know much about it. So you will have to do your homework and find out what you can about what you need and what kind of coverage is available.

The final kind of insurance involved with farming is crop insurance. Farmers purchase crop insurance as a risk management tool. If their crops are wiped out by a natural disaster, such as a tornado or a drought, they will still get something back on their investment. However, one of the reasons why farmers associate themselves with CSAs is to share the risks of farming; in that sense, the CSA itself is a form of crop insur-

Crop insurance, which farmers purchase to protect themselves in case of a natural disaster such as a tornado or flood, is not usually necessary for a CSA, where the members share the risks of farming (PHOTO: NANCY SULLIVAN)

ance. Members agree to accept what the CSA grows, and if there is a drought or storm that destroys some crops, everyone just gets a little less. On the other hand, if it's a great year, everyone gets a little more—it works both ways, and both the risk and the benefits are shared by the group.

If your urban farm project gets big enough, you may need to look into traditional crop insurance. The U.S. Department of Agriculture has involved itself in farm insurance for decades, and they provide information about the types of insurance available and how to find an agent or company to purchase the insurance you need. The Ohio Farmers Union is also a good resource for this type information.

Types of crop insurance available are listed at *www.rma.usda.gov/policies*, and the information at *http://www.rma.usda.gov/tools/agent.html* can provide you with help finding an insurance agent.

CHANGING THE WAY WE DO BUSINESS: SOMETHING TO THINK ABOUT

You will encounter difficulties in balancing your budget the first year, and probably in the second, third, and fourth years too. In our economy, people are often not willing to pay what fresh, organically grown food is really worth. Farm subsidies for corporate farms make it possible for them to charge less for their produce. Large chain grocery stores use fresh vegetables as a loss leader to bring people into the store to buy less healthy but more profitable processed foods. It's likely you will never be able to set the price of a CSA share at a level that covers all the costs of growing the food.

It is also difficult to pay farmers a reasonable wage, although they are often willing to work for a modest income. Using an intern system to have your professional farmer train new recruits is a way to keep staff expenses low while providing people with a great setting for learning how to farm. (People pay increasingly large fees to learn their occupations at universities, and they also pay

How your CSA operates, how it creates jobs, pays the staff, and trains interns, among other functions, reflects the social values of your organization—it's a way to change the world, beginning in your own community

to attend conferences or symposia to learn new techniques in their field, so there's no reason to feel guilty about providing low-cost or no-cost training to someone who wants to learn how to farm.) Creating such a training program will also help encourage more urban farming and more CSAs growing their food locally, so if you can train new farmers, your community and other communities will reap the benefits along with the fledgling farmers.

And it's a good start at changing our world, too. What we really want to do is to develop and demonstrate a new paradigm—a new way of living our lives—by creating relevant and useful jobs and simply living well with less. If we can begin to work outside the current economy, we can think about what is best for the farmer and how to make people see the worth in work like local farming.

On one hand, we'd like to be able to offer our staff benefits that most employees are accustomed to getting, such as workers' comp, health insurance, and unemployment insurance. On the other hand, these benefits can be no more than a patchwork of fixes for problems created by the current system—they don't get at the root of the issue of people employing other people. If we have a system that is based on the Earth as our primary concern—rather than money—maybe we wouldn't need these types of stopgap measures at all. Instead, we would have systems that simply take care of the Earth and its people directly.

This may be getting too philosophical for a chapter on the business side of the CSA, but we hope it gives you something to think about. We've started an urban farm project in our neighborhood to try a new way of doing things, growing our own food locally as a co-operative venture. It's working, so why not turn our attention next to the economy at large? Local food can create value chains that have an impact on our community. If that impact is big enough, maybe we can begin to seek changes in how our entire economy works. It's worth considering. ▪

Chapter 5

Growing Your Produce

We must cultivate our own garden.
—Voltaire

PLANNING TO PLANT

The most important thing you need to make your urban farm project successful is a knowledgeable farmer. The Enright Ridge CSA benefited from a skilled and experienced farmer to get our farm started, and we can't stress enough that although volunteers are the life's blood of our operation, you need at least one paid professional on staff. Farming is a serious undertaking, and you need someone who knows the ropes.

This chapter covers the basics of planning, planting, tending, and harvesting your crops, but it's no substitute for having a professional at the helm of your farm. The good news is there is a lot of help available, in the form of books, websites, and even county and university farm extension programs. So, if you know what you need to know, you can find information on almost any farming topic. The trick is knowing the questions so you can find the right answers:

Transplanting nursery starts in preparation for a new growing season (PHOTO: NANCY SULLIVAN)

- ▶ What kind of advance planning do we need to do?

- ▶ What kinds of crops should we grow?

- ▶ How much of each is enough?

51

- ▶ Should we buy or rent the equipment we need?
- ▶ What's needed to prepare beds for planting?
- ▶ How can we manage weeds and garden pests sustainably and, if possible, organically?
- ▶ What's involved in irrigating the crops beyond turning on the hose?

Planning for the Season and Keeping Good Records

Good planning is key to farming success. If you are just getting started in farming, you might want to start small as you are learning how things are done, and planning is the best way to make sure you don't overextend yourself. The planting guides in Appendix A (pp. 98–102) provide some examples you can use to plan how much to plant and when to plant it. You can also find yield tables in seed catalogs that will give you an estimate of how much produce you can expect to harvest. The production you'll see on your farm will vary, so it's important to start keeping good records from the very beginning. The information you log about what seeds you plant, the conditions you plant them in, when you plant, how much you harvest, and when you harvest it, will make it easier to plan for succeeding seasons.

How much you should plant to have enough food for the shareholders in your CSA depends on a number of variables:

- ▶ The size of the share—how many people is it intended to feed per week
- ▶ The variety of produce you want to provide and your members expect to get
- ▶ Popularity of certain items—you can probably plan on needing more tomatoes than celeriac, for example, because people know and like tomatoes, whereas celeriac is less known and people may not be clamoring for it
- ▶ Plan for crop failures; current wisdom suggests you plant about 20% more than you think you will need to cover losses during production to drought, heat, pests, and other calamities

Row covers protect early crops of greens from frost; plan on planting about 20% more than you will need to cover losses from inclement weather, insects, and other problems

Copyright © 2013 Enright Ridge Urban EcoVillage CSA

Table 5.1 Approximate Yield for Vegetable Crops per 15-Foot Row

Vegetable	Yield	Vegetable	Yield
Asparagus	4.5 Lbs	Lettuce, head	7 Lbs
Bean, lima (bush)	4 Lbs	Lettuce, leaf	7 Lbs
Bean, snap (bush)	15 Lbs	Muskmelon	15 Lbs
Beets	20 Lbs	Mustard greens	11 Lbs
Broccoli	11 Lbs	Okra	16 Lbs
Carrots	20 Lbs	Onion, bulb	17 Lbs
Cabbage	22.5 Lbs	Peas	3 Lbs
Cauliflower	15 Lbs	Pepper, bell	20 Lbs
Chard	11 Lbs	Potato, sweet	30 Lbs
Corn	18 Lbs (ears)	Potato, white	36 Lbs
Cucumber, slicing	21 Lbs	Spinach	10 Lbs
Cucumber, pickling	27 Lbs	Squash, summer	52 Lbs
Garlic	6 Lbs	Squash, winter	45 Lbs
Eggplant	15 Lbs	Tomato	42 Lbs
Kohlrabi	6 Lbs	Turnip	27 Lbs

Table 5.1 above provides some estimates about how much yield of different types of vegetables you will get from a 15-foot row. Keep your own records of approximate yield per bed or per row so you can plan more accurately in succeeding seasons.

Farm Algorithms

An algorithm is defined as a process or set of rules to follow in calculations or problem solving. In farming, this relates to the process of determining what to plant, how much to plant, and when to plant it. Some people work out algorithms by creating flowcharts that graphically express the steps in the process and what happens if variables are changed or a different decision is made. You can find more information about these kinds of algorithms in some of the references at the back of this book. Keep in mind that if you search for "farm algorithms" online, you will find a lot of off-topic pages about content farms and servers and other things that "grow" online rather than in a field. You will do better to search on "crop planning," and yes, you'll find that they even make software for that. (One popular program, for "small farmers and serious gardeners," that could easily be adapted to use in an urban CSA, is called simply *Cropplanning*.)

Another approach is to make a kind of "map" of your growing season. Table 5.2 on pages 54–55 is an example of a crop plan that shows what is planted and what is harvested in each week of the season, with estimated yields for each crop. Taking the time to make a crop plan like this will give you a reference point to check throughout the season as you farm.

Table 5.2 Crop planning spreadsheet, Part 1

Crop/variety x plant/harvest dates																						Harvest Period is in shaded area		Value in shaded area is weight per week for each share					
CSA Week Number																						1	2	3	4	5	6	7	8
Week of Year			5	6	7	8	9	#	11	12	13	14	15	16	17	18	19	20	21	22	23	24	25	26	27	28	29	30
Frost																													
Date			1/29	2/5	2/12	2/19	2/26	3/5	3/12	3/19	3/26	4/2	4/9	4/16	4/23	4/30	5/7	5/14	5/21	5/28	6/4	6/11	6/18	6/25	7/2	7/9	7/16	7/23
Spring vegetables		d\T							40				45	50				55	60	65			70					
D	Beet	red ace;J	50								P	P									0.75	0.75	0.75	0.75				
T	broccoli	Signal;J	50							S				T									1.00	1.00				
*	broccoli	Packman;J									S					T									1.25	1.25		
T	cabbage	Primax;J	60						S				T							0.50		0.50	1.50				

What to Plant

There are a lot of decisions involved in what to plant—you not only have to decide which kinds of produce to grow, but also what varieties of each kind you select. Keep your membership in mind when you make these decisions; will they try new and unusual vegetables, or is it better to stay with common and easily recognizable selections, such as green beans, tomatoes, carrots, and lettuce?

Some literature suggests that twenty different types of vegetables and greens, with several varieties of things like tomatoes and lettuce, is a good starting point for a moderate-size CSA. But there are farms that are offering twice that many selections in a CSA share over the course of a season. Determine what your members want, what you can grow in the space you have, and most importantly, what will grow in your climate.

If you have already done some farming, grow what you know! This will dovetail with what your land is good for growing. For example, if you are growing only in backyards to start, stick with tomatoes, herbs, radishes—things that grow well in small areas and raised beds. But if you have enough land, you can grow corn, pumpkins, and melons—all popular items.

Select seeds for varieties that will do well in your climate (you can find this kind of information in seed catalogs), and when you've become more experienced, you can try growing things that might be a little more risky in your area.

Most farms stick with annuals—plants that you grow from seed every year—but we recommend you look into perennials, too. These often require more of a commitment on the part of the farmer and the members, because it can take a season or more to establish perennial food crops such as berries, grapes, asparagus, and rhubarb. It's an even bigger commitment to think about apples, pears, peaches, and nuts, because the trees need to grow and

A homemade cold frame allows you to start crops from seeds before the growing season begins (Photo: Amy Matthews Stross/Hillside Community Garden)

Table 5.2 Crop planning spreadsheet, Part 2

You could use bunches or heads instead of lbs	Number of CSA shares													
	100													
Lbs/ share/ planting	Required yield/ planting	% store & handl loss	Required Yield lbs	Yield lbs/acre US ave.	Planted area in acres	Planted area in ft2	Linear feet bed space 5' bed	# rows on ~ 42" bed top	Between row inches	In row spacing inches	Number viable seed/plant	% loss germ, selection	Seeds per Oz	Amount Required in Oz.
					145x6'=0.02ac									
3.00	300	15	353	14,000	0.025	1,098	220	3	14	3	3765	0.2	1,600	2.82
2.00	200	15	235	9,500	0.025	1,079	216	2	21	15	493	0.2	9,000	0.07
2.50	250	15	294	9,500	0.031	1,349	270	2	21	15	617	0.2	9,000	0.082
2.50	250	15	294	23,500	0.013	545	109	2	21	15	249	0.2	9,000	0.033

establish themselves for years before you'll see any yield, but that doesn't mean they aren't worth growing. If your urban CSA is going to succeed, you're in it for the long haul. If you have the room to establish an orchard, by all means do so. And if you have less space, even a few berry canes or an asparagus patch is an investment in your farm's future.

If you don't have a greenhouse, you need other ways to start your seeds. Some crops can be grown directly from seeds in the bed, but for many other types of produce, you will plant seedlings started indoors or in cold frames, hoop houses, or some other protected space. Use the resources you have; you might ask for volunteers among your members who have space to start flats at their homes or find a place you can start seeds growing under lights.

And to find a source for those seeds, you can ask other farms where they buy seeds, look online for vendors (you might also find seed sellers at conferences geared toward small farmers), or try the *Suppliers of Seed for Certified Organic Production Database*. If you can find (or start) a seed exchange in your area, that's a good way to diversify the varieties you plant. There are even online seed exchanges where you can offer or request seeds for specific varieties.

DIG DEEPER

National Sustainable Agriculture Information Service, a program of the National Center for Appropriate Technology, maintains the seed database at https://attra.ncat.org/attra-pub/organic_seed/.

When to Plant and Succession Farming

Before you actually started farming, you may have thought of the process as planting in the spring, tending in the summer, and harvesting in late summer and fall. That doesn't work for a CSA, because members expect to get produce in their shares all season long. So, you have to plan to have items ready to harvest from the first week to the last of your season, which could be from four to eight months long, depending on your climate and your access to a greenhouse.

And to keep the produce coming, you'll have to do some succession planting, too—some crops, like lettuce and other greens, root vegetables, and beans, need to be planted more than once in a season. This is where making a planting schedule is very important—you need to map out your growing areas into beds or rows and determine what you will grow where, and when you will grow it. You may find that many times you will reseed or transplant seedlings into a bed not long after you harvest a crop of carrots or lettuce. For fast growing crops, you may continue the cycle of planting and harvesting and replanting many times in a season.

You need to know when you can start planting, so you can get early crops in as soon as possible. Knowing your spring frost dates will let you start greens and root vegetables that can stand a little cold and will also let you plan when to start putting in warm weather crops, which you may want to plant in waves, too, so that everything doesn't ripen at the same time. The goal is to have enough produce and enough variety, but to space out what is harvested throughout the entire season.

Some chilly weather crops that grow fast and well in the cool weather of spring may mature slower, with less yield, in the fall. You can find information about what grows well when, but some of it is going to be trial and error, seeing what does best during different seasons in your climate and your soil.

If you want to be able to do a lot of planting at one time, look into planting several varieties with different maturation dates—there are tomatoes that are ready to pick in about 60 days, and others that take 80 days or more to ripen; you can grow early and late sweet corn; and there are some greens that do better in spring and others that flourish in fall weather.

Although you need to have produce ready to pick every week, there are some crops, like green beans and peas, that are time-consuming to harvest, but it goes faster if there is plenty to pick. So, for these crops, it makes sense to plant more to ripen at the same time, for efficiency. You can remind your members that these legumes are easy to blanch and freeze if they get a lot in one share.

Radishes are just one example of a crop you can plant twice in a season, in the spring and in the fall

You also might want to plant more of certain crops or make additional plantings if you have problems with disease, insects, or drought, which may cause you to lose most or all of a harvest. Keep records so you can track problems and successes from season to season.

Make a planting schedule in the preseason and try to stick with it, even in the busy days of summer. Try to make planting as efficient as possible, too. Line up available workers in advance, keep tools available and ready to use, and arrange to have soil or bed preparation done in advance.

Also, you want to make sure you have enough seeds to get through the season. Not only can running out of seeds hold up planting, sometimes seeds may not even be available later in the growing season.

Here are a few examples of succession farming you can use to guide your planning:

▶ Plant once: tomatoes, potatoes, peppers, eggplant, leeks, onions, shallots, sweet potatoes, beans (pole), winter squash

▶ Plant two or three times: broccoli, cabbage, carrots, corn, cucumbers, melons, radishes (once in spring, once in fall), beets, brussel sprouts, scallions, summer squash

▶ Plant every two weeks: beans (bush), lettuce, salad mix

PRODUCTION PROCESSES

The next few sections briefly describe many of the tasks required to ensure that your urban farm project is successful, from preparing the soil to harvesting the crops. Find more detailed information that relates to your climate online or from experienced farmers in your area. When you know what questions to ask, there are plenty of ways to get the answers.

Soil Preparation/Fertility

Urban farming comes with its own set of concerns when it comes to the soil you'll be planting crops in. You have to worry about how acidic or basic it is, how sandy or loamy, if it's got too much clay content, just like farmers anywhere (more information about testing soil fertility is provided on page 25 in Chapter 3). But you also have to make sure it doesn't have high levels of lead and other heavy metals like cadmium and mercury. Soil in the city can be contaminated by air pollution, the exhaust from cars and factories, as well as from the debris of whatever might have been built on or near your farm plots in the past. And the contaminants in the soil can be taken up into the growing plants, making the produce toxic.

DIG DEEPER

Some good online sources that cover every aspect of farming for the beginner are *The Greenhorns Field Guide for Beginning Farmers*, at http://fieldguideforbeginningfarmers.wikispaces.com, and *Beginning Farmers*, at http://www.beginningfarmers.org.

Test your soil, and if it does have high levels of contaminants or the soil pH levels aren't the best for growing vegetables, there are a few things you can do to remediate it:

- ▶ The simplest solution is to use raised beds or container gardens, filled with untainted soil mix.

- ▶ Add compost and/or calcium to the soil to lower soil acidity, which will reduce the uptake of heavy metals by plants.

- ▶ Mix or cover the ground with clean, uncontaminated soil.

- ▶ Plant vegetables that grow fruit—such as peppers, eggplant, and tomatoes—instead of root vegetables or leafy plants like lettuce, which absorb heavy metals at higher levels.

If you find your soil is highly contaminated, you can't plant edible plants in it at all. There are ways to make the soil usable, growing cover crops that absorb the metals and then disposing of them, until the soil is usable—a worthy project but a long-term commitment.

On the other hand, if your soil tests okay for contaminants but is like most city plots, lots of fill and just not great soil for farming, you can add compost and other amendments to enrich it and provide needed nutrients for the growing plants.

Composting

Compost! Maybe you already are doing it, but do more if you can. Some municipalities have a lot of rules and laws that regulate large-scale composting enterprises, so do take time to check the legality in your community, but even when there are fairly stringent regulations, you

Use the vegetable waste generated by farming—dead plants, vegetable trimmings, and other plant material—as well as fallen leaves collected from your neighborhood to start composting (PHOTO: NANCY SULLIVAN)

can usually compost on your own property with your own material. There's always a lot of material around a farm—overripe produce, plants that are pulled after they have been harvested, and the offal of prepping the food for member shares all generate a lot of waste that won't go to waste if you've got a good compost pile.

There is plenty of information on composting available online and at your local library, and it doesn't take any special equipment to get started. Find a spot and turn the pile with a pitchfork occasionally, that's all you need to do. If your community allows, collect food scraps from restaurants in your area to add to your compost piles. It's a commodity you can create yourself, building rich soil to add nutrients to your vegetable beds.

Bed Preparation

And speaking of beds, you'll want to prepare your beds before planting seedlings. Most farmers will tell you that the soil is one of the most important aspects of a successful farm. You'll need to decide if you are going to plant directly in the ground or build raised beds. In an urban setting, if you are working on the site of an old industrial or public building, you might want to consider raised beds, because the soil onsite could be contaminated. If you do plant directly in the soil, you will want to get the soil tested, as explained previously.

After the soil is turned, you can add organic matter—compost or manure—digging it into the top 6 to 8 inches of ground, where it will help nurture the plants' roots. You also want the soil to be well aerated, not clumpy, to allow room for roots to grow and worms to travel. Check the moisture level, too; soil should be fairly dry for planting. Usually that's not a problem, but if you are trying to farm in a swampy area, you may need to dig drainage ditches to achieve the proper moisture levels.

If you have not farmed the land previously, you may not need to add any other amendments, because there will be plenty of unused nutrients in the soil. However, as you continue to farm in your urban area, you can find organic amendments that add nutrients or alter the pH of the soil, which you may want to do, depending on what crops you are planting.

WHAT'S THE BUZZ

When you build raised beds, you can fill them with the best soil mix for the crops you are planting. If you plant directly in the ground, you'll want to till the soil—many people recommend "double digging" new farm plots, first digging down about 12 to 18 inches and removing any rocks and roots.

Level the soil and rake it, and be sure to leave adequate space between beds so farmers and other workers can maneuver to weed, water, and harvest the crops. And remember, bed preparation is an ongoing task; you may need to amend the soil between crops, and though the beginning-of-the-season prep will be easier after the first year (all those rocks will be gone), you still need to turn the soil, rotate crops, and add nutrients through compost and other soil amendments.

Nursery

It's helpful to have a place to start seeds and grow seedlings until they are ready to be put out in the gardens. If you have a greenhouse or hoop house, you can grow more crops on less land because you will be able to have succession plantings in one garden. Other options for starting seeds in advance include simply constructed cold frames.

Of course, seeds can be planted directly in the ground, but having some kind of nursery facilities, even if they are fairly primitive, gives you several advantages, the most important of which is being able to grow several crops in one plot of land over the course of a season.

Tools and Equipment

You need tools to farm—shovels, rakes, pitchforks, and spades, not to mention hammers and screw-driver and drills if you are going to be building raised beds. Also, you will need some equipment, ranging from big containers for soil mix to trays for starting seedlings to hoses and drip lines, maybe a tiller or even a tractor.

There's some equipment you will likely have to buy, and you need to account for that in your budget, but many items will be a one-time expense and can be used for years, especially if they are well cared for. You can think about renting some larger equipment—saws for building raised beds or a tiller to turn beds can be affordable if you only have to pay for the use of it a day or two at a time. You may even be able to borrow that kind of equipment from another farm or from a CSA member.

You'll need a secure place to keep your tools and equipment, too; using part of a hoop house or green-house for storage makes sense; alternatively, you might build a small tool shed near where you farm to store CSA gear.

Pest Control

You don't want bugs on your plants, for the most part. Pollinators are fine, but pests are pests and you want to avoid them, or know how to get rid of them, without poisoning the environment—or yourself. The good news is that it is easier to learn organic practices from the start, rather than switching to them later. Research what crops you should grow together to ward off certain insects (companion planting), and consider crop rotation and insect habitats when you make your planting plans.

You have to plan ahead and

Keeping your crops bug-free begins before the first shoots appear, through good practices including preparing the soil to grow healthy plants and keeping them well watered and weeded

think in the long run to keep your crops free of blight and bugs. If you are doing the right things in other areas—proper bed preparation and amending the soil to keep it fertile, careful crop planning, and good practices keeping the crops irrigated and weed free—you have already won half the battle in pest control.

Irrigation

Your seedlings are planted, you are watching out for bugs and diseases and keeping ahead of the weeds, then it just stops raining for weeks—or months. This is going to happen (or else the reverse, you'll have a monsoon season), and most people would say the only thing to do is irrigate with water from a source near your beds.

But there are actually a few other choices, steps you can take to offset the effects of a drought on your crops—if you plan ahead. Some of these steps include the following:

- ▶ Conservation tillage (leaving the residue of the last crop, and the moisture that residue contains, on the fields or beds)

- ▶ Planting drought-resistant varieties

- ▶ Weed management (don't let the weeds take what water there is away from your crops)

Work Share Management

An urban co-operative CSA has a unique source of farm workers in its members. They signed up to work a certain number of hours to help grow their own food, and the trick is to make them efficient workers as quickly as possible, without distracting the farmer and other paid staff from their own work.

We have found that the best way to do this is to organize members into teams with team leaders who are responsible for making sure the work gets done, and they have members to do the work. It may take some experimenting to determine what your teams should be and how they should be organized. For example, in the first few seasons, we organized teams by the work that needed to be done: soil preparation, weeding and pest control, irrigation, and so on. But we were farming in quite a few different places, and eventually it became clear that it made more sense to organize by location. So now there are garden teams, and each team has enough workers to take responsibility for all the tasks required in a particular garden.

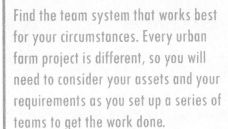

WHAT'S THE BUZZ

Find the team system that works best for your circumstances. Every urban farm project is different, so you will need to consider your assets and your requirements as you set up a series of teams to get the work done.

As another example of how our teams have evolved, we had an irrigation team that was responsible for watering the seedlings and plants in our greenhouse every morning and every evening through the growing season. This was a bit of work at first, as workers had to take the various hoses and make the rounds of the two sections of the building, one with starts and the other with growing crops, to make sure everything was watered sufficiently. Over the past few seasons, we've added a lot of drip lines to make watering the crops more efficient—now it's just a matter of turning a spigot, and the greenhouse crops are watered. So, the team has evolved into the greenhouse care team, with additional responsibilities that had previously been done by other teams.

The goal is to create teams that work for your circumstances. Having team leaders who check in with the staff and then let the members of each know what work needs to be done when, and where, makes the farmer's job easier. You may even want to consider having a work team coordinator who can help make sure that the work is getting done and members are getting work hours in. We've also experimented with using the social media platform Twitter to post general announcements about work days and tasks.

Some of the farming tasks require a little training, and others might need supervision by a staff member, and it's important that you address both of these aspects of co-operative farming. There's nothing more frustrating for either side, staff or workers, than to be put into a position where you don't know what you are doing and can't find anyone to help explain what you need to know. It's a good idea to have a couple of training sessions led by a team leader or staff member to explain the basics, and with cell phones in every pocket these days, having a contact for workers to call to get more information if needed is another way to get more work done with less trouble and dissatisfaction.

Team members often come back and do the same jobs season after season, and if they know and like the work they are doing, that is even more likely to happen. Provide orientation for new members and training for anyone starting a new chore, and make sure you have a way for people to contact staff with any problems that arise, and you will have a happy and productive work force.

We use a simple system of forms in a binder for members to track their hours, but there are plenty of different ways you can do this, too, from a computerized system to a chart or other visual method. Again, you may find the way that works best for your CSA by trial and error, as you find what works best, and what doesn't work at all.

Harvest

Finally, we've arrived at the best part of urban farming—harvest! This is a task that happens every week, determining what is ready to pick to give all the members of the CSA a share of the produce. The farmer has planned the planting and variety of crops to make sure there are things ready to harvest every week, from greens and herbs and root vegetables in the earliest days to tomatoes and peppers and squash in the middle of summer, and back to greens and root vegetables at the end of the growing season.

The farmer is also the one who will determine what gets picked each week for shares. Harvesting is a task that members can do, but they will need supervision and training, at least at first. Another issue with harvesting is timing it—you need to pick the week's produce as close to pickup time as possible, but you also need to have enough time to get it picked, cleaned, and packed or displayed, according to how you provide your shares to members.

If you have your pickup on Saturday mornings, as we do, that means harvesting on Fridays. That's a workday for a lot of people, and in fact, this is an issue that comes up a lot with a co-operative farm. There is

The farmer must work out what is ready to be harvested each week, and crops should be picked as close to the pickup time as possible—usually no more than the day before for most vegetables

work to do every day, but a lot of people in the CSA work regular Monday through Friday jobs, and there is only so much work that can be done in the evenings and on weekends. Members who work irregular hours or who have evening/weekend jobs will probably be in the minority, but you should encourage them to get their hours in when less workers are available.

It's best to harvest early in the day, when it is cooler, but you will need to arrange your harvest hours around when volunteers or staff members are available

We do depend on staff to do a lot of the harvesting, but we've also experimented with harvesting in the early evening on Fridays, to get some of the after-work crowd. That works better in the spring and fall than in the heat of the summer, when the hottest part of the day can be late afternoon and early evening. It's a matter of matching up the work with available workers, and knowing in advance how much help you will need to harvest the week's produce.

After harvesting, the produce is the responsibility of the packout team, who handle the logistics of cleaning, counting, sorting, displaying, and/or packing up the food for the week's share, which is covered in the next chapter.

From planting to harvest, the growing process is time-consuming, labor intensive, and has many different tasks to coordinate, but it's the heart of the CSA. And what comes after harvest—enjoying meals made with fresh, locally grown produce—makes all the advanced planning and hard work worth it! ∎

Chapter 6

Distributing Your Produce

Copyright © 2013 Enright Ridge Urban EcoVillage CSA

We learn from our gardens to deal with
the most urgent question of the time:
How much is enough?
—Wendell Berry

Afer you have planted your crops, cared for them, and harvested the produce, there is still one more step in the process of urban farming: You must get what you have grown to your members. When you make your distribution plan, keep your options open, because you may find that you need to refine the plan after you see it in action.

You need to find a place and set a schedule for picking up shares, and you should set up a procedure and make sure members are aware of it—and that they are aware of the consequences of not following the procedure.

ORGANIZING A PICKUP PLACE AND SCHEDULE

There are many ways you can set up distribution; every farm should find the method that works best for their own situation. Make it as well-organized as you can manage with the resources you have, and try to find the quickest way to get the produce to your members—the least time required for the farm staff and volunteers, so they can concentrate their time on farming, and the most efficient setup for members picking up their shares.

Pickup day for your CSA should be well-organized and convenient for volunteers and staff who are setting things up for distribution as well as for members who are coming to get their shares of the produce

Finding a Location

A location close to or at the place you are farming is best, because you don't have to move the crops a long distance after harvest. You need some kind of protected space with room for storage and room for pickup. The Enright CSA uses an old florist shop attached to our greenhouse for distribution, and it is an ideal situation—it is near our gardens and it has a walk-in cooler for storage, running water to clean vegetables, and a large space to set up the food in baskets and bins.

But there are alternatives in your own community, too. You may find a church or school that has a cooler (or a basement room) where you can store produce for a day or two, and you can distribute shares from a space in a public building, a hoop house, a garden shed, or a member's garage or porch. You could even distribute shares from picnic tables set up under pop-up canopies if necessary.

Whatever your location, keep in mind that it needs to be safe and convenient for your members. Some things to consider when you are choosing a distribution site include:

▶ Check traffic patterns for vehicles coming and going, and parking for people while they are picking up their shares. If your members all come from a nearby area, you may be able to convince some of them to come to pickup on foot or by bicycle, but many people will still come by car, so you need to plan for that.

- ▶ Provide some kind of shelter with adequate light and ventilation, and with tables or shelves to hold the produce, whether it is pre-packed for members or arrayed for them to pack up themselves.

- ▶ Keep liability issues in mind—make sure you have insurance coverage for any injuries or accidents that might happen during pickup at your site.

- ▶ Set up the pickup area so it looks appealing and keep it as clean as possible.

- ▶ Make sure your members get the information they need at pickup about what they are getting, how much they are getting, and even suggestions about what to do with the produce. Distribute a weekly newsletter or use signs and bulletin boards to keep members well informed.

Setting a Schedule

Our CSA has a share pickup once a week during the six-month growing season and members pick up their produce on Saturday mornings. This works well for us, but if you have a lot of members or your crops are not all likely to ripen at the same time, you might set up a staggered schedule, with some members coming on Wednesday and some on Saturday, for example. Other CSAs are set up so that only half the members pick up each week.

Your schedule will be determined to an extent by your pickup location and your members' schedules. If most of your shareholders work during the week, having pickup on a Thursday morning is not going to make sense. And if you are using a church hall for distribution, you are not going to want to set your pickup time for Sunday mornings. The important thing when setting the schedule is to make it convenient for both the workers and the members; remember, you want to keep your members happy so they'll return the next season, and if pickup is always a drag, they may think twice about continuing to belong to the CSA.

Pickup is a great time to create good feelings about your urban farm. People who stop in to get their shares at the Enright CSA also take time to see what is growing in the gardens out back and to talk to fellow members. A lot of recipes are exchanged during pickup, and we encourage socializing by sometimes having baked goods and tea or coffee, with music playing at background level. The binder we use to track work hours is always available during pickup hours so people can keep their forms up to date, and there are usually posters and flyers about upcoming community events on the greenhouse's walls and windows. It's a convivial atmosphere that allows people to linger and talk if they want to, but we have enough space that the socializing usually doesn't get in the way of the business of pickup.

Box or Buffet?

How will your members get their produce? You'll have to decide if it's best to have pre-packed shares ready or let people put together their own shares. The majority of CSAs box up everything a member receives at pickup and has shares ready and waiting. That's not how we do it, however. Our pickup procedure has been to have a packout team with members who arrive early on Saturday morning to get the produce ready by counting or weighing what has been harvested, washing it as necessary, and then displaying it on tables in the distribution area, creating a kind of buffet where people pack their own shares into bags they bring with them each week. Each kind of produce has a sign indicating how much members should take for their shares.

WHAT'S THE BUZZ

If you use boxes (or some other kind of containers) to pack shares in advance, you need to have at least two containers per share—one will be at the member's house and the other at the distribution site. And you have to depend on the members to bring back their empty boxes every week.

Boxed Shares

The benefits of pre-packed shares are:

▶ It's easy to make sure everyone gets their fair share, even if there are shortages of some produce. Workers can use a mix-and-match system to deal with shortfalls.

▶ It's the simplest and quickest method for members, who just have to pick up their box and go.

Drawbacks for this method include:

▶ There is little or no choice for the members in what they get or don't get; this may cause waste in the long run.

▶ It's more trouble and takes more time to pack up everyone's share in advance.

Pack It Yourself

For the buffet style, the benefits are:

▶ There is more member choice (to a point) in what to take or not take.

▶ It's easier and quicker for workers to set out large bins of produce.

▶ No need to provide boxes or baskets; members bring their own bags.

▶ It provides more opportunity for members to meet and talk about how to prepare the produce.

Some of the drawbacks include:

▶ You need enough space to set out all the produce and have room for members to walk through and pick out their share, as well as room for people who want to stay and chat.

▶ There's a need for supplies such as rubber bands and small plastic bags for loose items and scales for produce that is divided up by weight.

▶ It takes longer for a member to come and pack up a share than to just pick up a box.

We use two shifts of packout workers for distribution. The first team works from 8:00 am to 10:30 am, getting the produce set out and determining how much each member will get. They display the produce in bins and baskets and make the signs that clip onto the containers with clothespins. We also have a large whiteboard where all the items in the week's share are listed so people can quickly and easily see what they are getting. The first shift begins the cleanup by tidying up the area where they work.

The second shift of workers comes at 10:00 am and stays until about 12:30 pm.

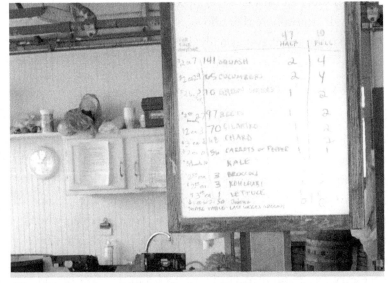

The whiteboard at right lists the items in the weekly share and how much of each type of produce is included in each share

They are there to interact with the members as they come in, and they make sure each member checks his/her name off the pickup list so we know who has (or hasn't) picked up a share. They also answer questions, provide bags as needed, help people with the scales, and generally act as the farm's goodwill ambassadors to the members. After noon, when pickup is officially ended, they pack up any leftover produce for storage in the cooler, mop the floor, and clean the tables, so the distribution area is ready for the next week.

One other responsibility of the second shift is to pack up shares for people who have let us know in advance that they won't be able to make the pickup time. This is a service we decided to offer; people often leave their own bags at the greenhouse with a note, or else they email the packout team leader by the night before pickup. Packed shares are put in the cooler for members to pick up later on Saturday or during the day on Sunday. On Monday morning, any shares that have not been picked up are disposed of. This system can be abused by thoughtless people, but for the most part, it has worked for us.

Delivery

Some CSAs provide delivery of shares, either to a few centrally located pickup sites or directly to members. This is certainly convenient for members, but it is probably not an efficient way for you to distribute your produce. If your urban farm is small, direct delivery to members might work, but it adds effort, and unless you have a fleet of bicycle carts, it also adds a lot to the farm's carbon footprint.

The point of an urban farm is to grow food in areas where people already are living and working, so no one should have too far to travel to pick up shares at a distribution site. We don't recommend offering delivery unless there are some extenuating circumstances. For example, if there are disabled or very elderly people in the neighborhood who are interested in participating, arrangements could be made for a member who lives nearby to deliver their produce to them. But for standard distribution, delivery probably doesn't make sense.

Beets and carrots are bundled for easier distribution of equal shares

WHAT'S IN A SHARE?

How do you know how much each member gets in their share, either to pack it up in advance or to let people know how much of each item to take from the produce buffet? This is where your math skills get a workout. You have to calculate how much you have of each item and divide it by the number of shares. This is easier with cabbages and squash than with beans and basil, obviously. Our packout members count vegetables like ears of corn, bunches of

Copyright © 2013 Enright Ridge Urban EcoVillage CSA

lettuce, turnips, and beets. We weigh tomatoes, beans, and herbs, setting the scale to discount the weight of the container these items are in.

Then it's just a matter of basic division (you might want to have a calculator handy at the distribution site, but it's also likely that every worker's phone has a calculator app). If you have 100 pounds of tomatoes, and you have 42 members, then every share will include a little less than 2½ pounds of tomatoes.

Label Your Produce

Now you know how much of each item everyone can take, but members are not necessarily going to know what every item is. There are, for example, a seemingly endless variety of greens, and people want to know if they are getting collards or kale or vitamin greens. They may never have heard of celeriac or yukina, so it's a good idea to clearly label the produce with the name of the item as well as how much to take. We try to put a list of expected harvest in our weekly newsletter, which we send out by email the day before pickup, and there is often an article about one of the vegetables in our newsletter or on our blog. These are all ways to keep members happy and coming back for more. If they know what they have and how to cook it, they will find they are getting greater value from their shares.

The Share Table

Every week at the Enright Ridge CSA greenhouse during pickup, you will hear the following kinds of conversations:

"Kale! Great, we haven't had that in months and it's my favorite."

"Really? You couldn't pay me to eat kale. If I take it, that will go straight to the compost bin."

"More cucumbers? I still have six from last week, what am I going to do with those?"

"Oh, I'd take all the cucumbers I can get. I make pickles for the whole family!"

And so on. That's where the share table comes in handy. If there is something in the share you don't want, leave it on the table for someone who will use it. And you are welcome to take what you can use in addition to your regular share.

We also put produce that is just starting to come in or beginning to taper off on the share table if there is not enough to give every member some. We have great farmers and amazing production processes, so we rarely have

> **WHAT'S THE BUZZ**
>
> The share table is a good way to eliminate waste on both ends, at the farm and in members' kitchens.

The share table lets people leave what they won't use so other folks can make good use of it

too little produce and have not had to set limits on the share table. However, if you have limited quantities, you can use the share table to even things out. Add up the number of items you have on the table (bags of beans, bunches of carrots, heads of cabbage) and divide it by the number of members in your CSA. Then hang a sign that tells people how many items they can take from the share table that week.

GAP AND GHP STANDARDS FOR PRODUCE

An urban CSA has the same responsibility as any restaurant, farmers' market, or green grocer to provide safe, fresh food. Good Agricultural Practices (GAP) and Good Handling Practices (GHP) focus on best agricultural practices to make sure that fruits and vegetables are produced, packed, handled, and stored in the safest manner possible to minimize risks of microbial food safety hazards.

There are food-handling classes available at many community colleges. These are often geared more toward restaurant workers, but the basics of food safety apply to any situation. You will also find that there are efforts made by government agencies and university extension programs to inform farmers of current safe agricultural practices. The Ohio State University's Fruit and Vegetable Safety Team offer a GAP education program, with workshops held in locations around the state.

The production and packout team members need to be aware of basic food safety procedures; GAP and GHP manuals and classes are available through The Ohio State University extension program

DIG DEEPER

Visit http://producesafety.osu.edu/ for more information about OSU's GAP workshops.

GAP and GHP standards involve several categories of possible contaminants: chemical (e.g., pesticides and additives); biological (e.g., animal or human pathogens); and physical (e.g., foreign objects). The areas that have potential for contaminating the produce include water (everything from irrigation to flooding to washing the harvested produce); soil amendments (compost, manure, or anything else added to the soil to improve its biology or add nutrients for the growing plants); handling practices (farm workers who harvest, wash, store, weigh, and pack the food); and traceability (not a source of pathogens, but the method that allows the source of an illness to be determined).

Safe food handling procedures start in the garden and continue into the distribution area, where workers must know how to clean and store the produce properly

There are many other elements to safe food handling, including storing produce at appropriate temperatures and in proper conditions; soil testing; appropriate plumbing and wastewater handling; risk assessment; keeping animals out of the fields and/or storage facilities. It's a lot to take in, but it's important for you to learn what you can about safe agricultural and food-handling practices from the start of your urban farm. There are many online sources of information where you can find best practices, and it is a good idea to have someone from your CSA take a GAP workshop or other food safety class early in the planning process for your organization.

CSA POLICY FOR PICKUP AND NON-PICKUP

You've set a pickup schedule, have a clean, well-lighted distribution spot, and keep your members informed of what's being harvested and when to pick up their shares. And yet some folks still don't show up to get their produce. How do you handle this? The best way to deal with missed pickups is to set a policy right from the beginning and stick with it.

Sometimes emergencies crop up; other times people go on vacation and completely forget about pickup day. There are also other concerns, such as people who always come right at the end—or after—pickup time, or who make arrangements to pick up their produce at a different time again and again and again, taking advantage of CSA workers and staff.

Depending on your circumstances, you may be able to accommodate people who come late or on another day, or you may not. The best way to approach it is to try to put as much of the responsibility on the members as possible. With our ubiquitous cell phones, a member can always call a friend or family member to make the pickup at the last minute.

That can cause its own problems, because the friend will not be familiar with the routine, though we do ask members to inform whoever is picking up for them how pickup protocol works. We have also found that having workers to assist newcomers can pay off; if their experience is good, you may have a potential new CSA member.

Remind people about pickup times in your communications, and if you have a chronically late member, try to make it clear that you have volunteers manning the distribution location, and they want to go home and get on with their Saturday (or Tuesday evening or whenever), rather than waiting around for latecomers. Set some basic policies about late and missed pickups and stick to them as much as possible. Following are a few examples of pickup policies we have established at the Enright Ridge CSA:

CSA PICKUP POLICY

▶ It is the responsibility of each member to pick up his/her weekly distribution of produce at the designated site and time. If you arrive late, your share may not be available for that week.

▶ Members agree to follow the instructions of the packout crew in collecting the quantity/amount and variety of produce included in the share each week.

▶ If a member is unable to pick up his/her share during a vacation or for any other reason, there are several alternative arrangements possible:

  ▶ Designate another person to pick up the share (making sure that the person is aware of pickup times and protocol).

  ▶ Alert the packout coordinator by e-mail by a set time that you want your share packed up and placed in the cooler for retrieval later.

  ▶ Let the packout coordinator know via e-mail by a set time that you will not be picking up a share so it can be added into the shares for other members.

There are many different ways to set up distribution. The main thing to remember is not to make it any more complicated than it needs to be. Keep it simple and efficient, and it will be a good experience for your members—as well as not too much of a burden for your workers. Pickup is the time when members can interact with each other and find out what's going on at the farm. Make it a fun and pleasant experience. That's one of the best ways to keep everyone in your urban CSA happy and satisfied. ■

WHAT'S THE BUZZ

Late pickup service (leaving pre-packed shares in a cooler for people who can't make the regular pickup time) is only possible if you have a public or open area where the produce is safe but available to members without requiring CSA staff in attendance.

Chapter 7

Communications

*The single biggest problem in
communication is the illusion
that it has taken place.*
—George Bernard Shaw

Communication is an important part of the business side of an urban farm, but it's also part of what puts the "community" in community-supported agriculture. We have to talk to each other to set up work teams, committees, schedules, and fundraising events, and we need to have clear and simple channels of communication. The goal is to use these channels to make the CSA function efficiently, which will create that sense of community, as we share a sense of accomplishment in growing our own food.

The question is how to communicate. Today, a lot of information is transmitted on the Internet, but for the first three years of our CSA, we did not really have an online pres-

Building community is a significant aspect of an urban CSA

73

ence. We had a page on the website of our parent organization with some information about share prices and contact information. For the most part, we communicated with members fairly effectively through emails and a newsletter that was sent by email and available in paper form at our Saturday pickup. We've also had a blog since the first year, so we have used electronic communication from the start. We greatly expanded that in our fourth year, and it has led to faster and easier communication in the long run, although it took some effort to set up the systems.

KEEPING IN TOUCH WITH CSA MEMBERS

Your urban CSA needs a membership committee to attract and retain members, but the communications team is also important, since everyone needs to know what is going on from week to week to stay involved and interested in the community farm.

The communications team for an urban CSA often works closely with many other teams, including the membership team, the work teams, and the social team. They may also work with the people who are doing fundraising to create announcements or flyers for special events.

We now communicate with members electronically with a website, email, a blog, Facebook, and Twitter, but we also retain some more traditional ways of letting people know what is going on, with a printed version of the newsletter still available on Saturday mornings at pickup, as well as various signs, posters, displays, cards, and brochures and flyers that we have to pass out to potential members.

Our CSA also sponsors monthly potluck dinners where members can meet and share recipes. After the dinner, we have a brief meeting or we socialize. Although electronic communication is effective and sometimes instantaneous, we've found that you can't beat a little face time among members to let people get to know one another and learn about how the CSA runs.

MAINTAINING AN ONLINE PRESENCE

Communication requires a small but hard-working team to cover all the bases. People with different skill sets can provide written material, logos and designs for printed brochures and a website, and of course you'll need people with those computer skills (or you'll have to plan to pay someone to design and set up a website).

The good news is that the electronic infrastructure really only needs to be set up one time; after that, it's a matter of maintaining and updating what you have in place. Getting the site set up may take time, depending on your vision and your expertise. There are simple ways to set up modest websites (WordPress, for example), some more complicated ways (registering a domain then setting up a site yourself using a web host), and some quite elaborate ways (hiring a web design firm to take care of the whole project for you—which may be less complicated but more expensive in the long run).

Whichever way you choose, you'll need to do a few things in advance:

▶ Decide what information you want to put online

▶ Write copy to provide text for the website

▶ Find some good images of your CSA (or use stock images) to get your message across—the Internet is a visual medium, so you don't want a lot of blocks of text because people won't take the time to read it all.

You'll also need to decide who will do the updates and maintenance. Another thing to remember is to make someone responsible for paying any fees associated with domain name registration and website hosting each year. It's a good idea to get websites and other online information set up in the off season; then the renewal will also come around in the off season when you have time to deal with it.

What to Put on Your Website

There are simple ways to create good-looking websites, and less is more in most cases. It's important to update sections of the website regularly—at least once a month is good. Calendars are useful, especially if you have meetings, regular work days, and pickup days to include, as well as:

▶ An About page that describes your CSA, its history, and what it has to offer

▶ A Contact page with how to contact someone from the CSA to join or find out more

▶ A Member page for announcements

▶ A Frequently Asked Questions page (this will save you a lot of emails and phone calls)

▶ A CSA Policy page (it's important for your CSA to set standard policy about things such as payments, work hours, missed pickups, and so forth)

▶ A page with an application to join the CSA (or a link to CSA management software that handles accounts)

DIG DEEPER

Examples of items in a CSA policy statement are shown on pages 71 and 86, and CSA management software is explained on page 88 in Chapter 8.

PICKUP AT
THE GREENHOUSE
EVERY SATURDAY
10:00 am - 12:00 pm

Find us on Facebook   Visit our Blog

Enright Ridge Eco-Village CSA
Price Hill's Urban Agriculture Project

HOME

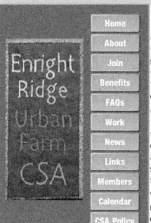

Home
About
Join
Benefits
FAQs
Work
News
Links
Members
Calendar
CSA Policy

Community supported agriculture.

Community supported agriculture (CSA) is way of sustaining farming and farmers, often in urban areas. Consumers who are interested in safe, wholesome food come together to support a farm operation, creating a community farm in which all the "share holders" share the risks and benefits of food production on a local level.

CSAs take many forms, and the Enright Ridge CSA was formed in 2009 as a work co-op, with members sharing the work of growing food in backyards and community gardens in the Price Hill area of Cincinnati. Our CSA has grown each year, adding more land and more members. We are currently growing produce more than six months a year, feeding about 150 people with garden and farm plots that add up to about an acre of land.

We are continuing to grow, adding more land and more members. Our goal is to continue our own success with this community-based urban agriculture project, while working to

Find us on Facebook

Enright Ridge Urban EcoVillage CSA

The Enright Ridge CSA website home page includes navigation buttons and a Facebook page feed

Other useful pages include:

▶ Links to current and past newsletters

▶ Calendar of upcoming events

▶ Links to other community organizations in your neighborhood

▶ Links to local food groups in your area

And you will probably find that there is information specific to your urban CSA that you want to include. Selecting a website host and software that allow you to build on to your website as you go is a good idea, because you will want to modify the site over time.

It can be difficult to delegate work on the website, especially if you use proprietary software to maintain it, but it's also within the scope of one person's volunteer time to be responsible for the website. It's a good idea to share the online responsibilities by having different volunteers take care of different aspects of electronic communication, such as email, blogging, and management software, rather than trying to have several people responsible for overlapping electronic spheres of influence. If you have some people who have special skills, such as writing, photography, or illustration, you can get them involved as well, providing content for your website and blog.

Communicate Efficiently by Email

Communicating via email is vital these days. (You probably don't want to have to take time to make telephone calls unless absolutely necessary.) If you have any non-email users, be sure to make paper copies of your newsletter available, and/or use a bulletin board at pickup for announcements, but most important notifications will go by email.

You can use automatic email systems to send out reminders of work days, pickup, meetings, payments due, and other regularly scheduled events. Search for information about setting up automatic emails online, ask about your website host's capabilities in this area, or depend on tech-savvy members. CSA management software also provides the ability to send out scheduled email automatically when someone joins, makes a payment, or takes other actions involving the management software.

Our CSA has some regularly scheduled events every month, including a potluck dinner and certain meetings. We need to remind all of our members of the potluck, and the members who are on committees need advance notice of regular meetings. To do this, we've set up a standard email that goes out one week before each event, with another that is sent the day before as a final reminder. We use a whole-group email to send the potluck reminders to every member, but we send the committee meeting reminders only to the members who are on that committee and whose email addresses are in a separate contact group. We use a program called Boomerang to set up the emails at the beginning of each month; you can find information about it and other email scheduling programs online.

DIG DEEPER

The Boomerang website is at www.boomeranggmail.com.

It's important to have an up-to-date and accurate list of email addresses for your members. Ask for email addresses on your application and use a reliable program to maintain the list. CSA management software will also maintain a current email list. If possible, use a flag or tagging system to indicate which members are associated with certain work teams or committees to send out emails to specific people.

Reach Members with a Blog

A blog is a simple way to interact with and inform your members. Although it can be used for announcements and news, it's also a way for members to share information among themselves, with recipes and preparation tips and news about other events at the CSA or in the community, and it might even be a place to post an inspiring poem or photograph.

Photos are important on the blog—images speak louder than words on the Internet. If you post a recipe, post a picture of the prepared dish. If you don't have one, look for a copyright-free or public domain photo that will suit the subject matter. You can find photos you can use without copyright restrictions at many sites, including Wikimedia Commons, Microsoft Office Images, and Public Domain Images.

DIG DEEPER

Look for stock photos on Wikimedia Commons at commons.wikimedia.org, Microsoft Office Images at www.office.microsoft.com, and Public Domain Images at www.public-domain-image.com.

Remember that not all image files work for a blog or a website—look for .jpg or .png file extensions to be sure the images will appear correctly online. If you have members with photography skills, ask them to take digital photographs of the work, produce, and events at the CSA for use online. Photos for a website or blog should be 72 dpi (dots per inch) resolution and image files should be fairly small, but not too small. A good rule of thumb is to keep the file size of images under 50K (kilobytes) so they don't take excessively long to load.

You can take your own photographs to illustrate your CSA website, or blog, or use stock photos from sites such as Wikimedia Commons

When cropping and resizing an image, to work out the approximate size you want the image to appear, multiply the number of inches by 72. This will give you the dimensions in pixels, the numerical value used by HTML code. For example, if you want an image to be about 4 inches high by 6 inches wide, the pixel height and width will be 288 by 432.

Update your blog year round and as often as you can (though of course it will have more entries in season than out). We post something every other day on average during the six months we are growing and picking up produce; in the other six months, we post a few times a month. Some ideas for blog posts:

▶ News about the planting, harvest, or improvements at your CSA

▶ Articles or news from elsewhere that support urban agriculture and the CSA model

▶ Seasonal information

▶ Recipes, recipes, recipes—ask for submissions, look online and in cookbooks (do give credit when recipes from elsewhere are used)

The setup time for a blog is minimal; you can go to a blogging site such as WordPress or Blogger and choose a design and a layout and set it up in just a few minutes. Anyone who is designated as an administrator of the blog can post items, and your members (and others) can choose to follow the blog. Anyone can add comments (they will probably need to sign in with an email address), and it's good to write blogs occasionally that encourage comments, by asking for ideas on how to prepare certain kinds of produce, for example.

Remember that everything online is interconnected, so be sure to put a link to your website on your blog, and a link to your blog on your website.

Social Media

Social media is so much a part of many people's lives today that you can't ignore it. Businesses, churches, schools, bands, and farms all have Facebook pages so you can "like" them, but we've found that our Facebook page also really does create an online community of members who share preparation tips, ask questions, and talk about the great meals they've prepared with CSA produce. It seems like social media and related online ways to advertise and promote your cause, group, or business multiply every day.

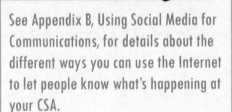

DIG DEEPER

See Appendix B, Using Social Media for Communications, for details about the different ways you can use the Internet to let people know what's happening at your CSA.

One social media site to mention in particular is Earthineer. It's a social site specifically geared toward folks who are interested in sustainable living—like you, if you are helping to establish an urban CSA. It's been described as "Facebook for farmers, but way more interesting." It's got blogs and there is a barter-share-trade feature, as well as the standard post-and-comment format like Facebook. And it has local roots—Dan Adams, who started Earthineer, is a graduate of Northern Kentucky University. He announced the startup at a talk at the university in 2010. Join at www.earthineer.com to see what it has to offer.

USING TRADITIONAL FORMS OF COMMUNICATIONS

Electronic communication is important, but you don't want to forgo traditional forms of sharing information. There are still a few good old-fashioned ways you will need to communicate with your members.

Information at Pickup

Your CSA will have a regularly scheduled place and time for members to pick up their share each week—take advantage of this to communicate information. Have copies of a weekly newsletter available, and post important information at pickup, too. We have some signs and other information that change from week to week but there is also information that is always posted to remind members about CSA policy and activities. We have a rack with magazines and flyers of interest as well as a bookshelf of donated books that operates as an honor lending library.

Newsletters   We e-publish a weekly newsletter during the growing season, and we print a few copies and have them available at our weekly pickup. The newsletter has an editor who takes submissions from members or writes articles to fill up the two-page format. It's not so much news as reminders and interesting tidbits. It's kind of funny, and it's colorful (though we print it in black and white, so you can only see how colorful it is if you read it online).

We can always use more submissions, but people do send in announcements of local events, recipes, and comments on what has been in past newsletters. We create our newsletter in Microsoft Publisher, although Microsoft Word or another word-processing or desktop publishing program could be used just as well. Then we make it into a PDF file, which makes it easier to print and to upload to our website (a simple procedure using the File Manager on any website provider).

DIG DEEPER

You can see an archive of Enright CSA weekly newsletters at http://www.enright-csa.org/gazettearchives.html.

After it is posted, we update our website with a new link to the new edition (an archive list on the Newsletter page lets people see previous issues). Then we send out a group email (we use Gmail) to let everyone know the new edition is available. This takes no more than a half-hour every week and is a discrete task that can be assigned to a communications team member with moderate computer skills if the newsletter editor cannot or does not want to handle that part of it.

Bulletin Boards A bulletin board at your pickup location is a good tool for timely messages to CSA members. We use whiteboards to provide information about work locations and activities, and we also use one to list the week's harvest. Any information that changes frequently but needs to be displayed prominently for people to see when they come for their share can be communicated well with conspicuously placed notices on these kinds of boards.

A sign clearly indicating the type of produce and amount per share

Signs and Notes Our CSA puts out the various kinds of produce in the share each week, with small signs clipped to the baskets and other containers that lets people know how much to take per share. This works well for us and our signs are eye-catching and communicate well, because we're lucky enough to have someone whose day job is in design as our pickup team leader. But the main thing you want to do is be clear and concise, so you don't have dozens of people asking if you really mean 1 pound of okra, not 1 okra, or similar questions.

If your CSA packs up shares in advance for members to pick up, put a note or newsletter in each packed share. A list of what's included is helpful, especially if there are things that the members might not be familiar with (various kinds of greens, for example). You can also include notices of upcoming events or work opportunities or other information.

Flyers and Brochures

We use a variety of different printed materials to promote our CSA to potential new members. We have a nice three-fold, full-color brochure that we print on a color printer, updating it each season with information about share costs and how to apply to become a member. We also have business cards that simply direct people who are interested to our website, where they can find the same information.

We have several different flyers that we pass out at neighborhood events and ecological, sustainable living, and outdoor events and festivals. Some of these are simple, directing people to our website through a QR code (short for "quick response code," explained in more detail in Appendix B); others are event-specific or feature a promotion. For example, one season we offered people a bonus of five work hours earned in advance if they sent in their application and deposit by a certain date. You could include a coupon for a discount on the price of a share on a flyer as well.

We create PDF files as finished artwork for flyers and brochures to make it easy to share the files, so people who need print materials can print copies as needed and we don't print more than we need. We use some of these flyers and brochures during the off-season, especially in the months leading up to the start of a new growing season, when we are actively courting new members for our CSA. We've found that setting up a booth or table at local green events, such as a wildflower festival and Earth Day celebrations in April, is a way to distribute information about our urban CSA to an audience predisposed to be interested in what we are doing.

Displays

When we have volunteers to attend green events around town, they set up a table with information about how the CSA works. Trifold display boards are available at local hobby shops and school supply stores, and you can find a crafty volunteer or two among your members to create a nice eye-catching display. Don't clutter the boards too much, and don't use too much text on the boards. Lean toward images and short, simple phrases—keep the longer descriptions of how the CSA works for your brochure or direct people to your website.

One more way to make another kind of display to promote your CSA is to get t-shirts or cloth carrier bags, either silk-screened (this could be costly, unless you happen to have a silk screen artist among your members who is looking to fulfill a work requirement) or done with iron-on images. Office supply stores sell iron-on paper that can be printed on an inkjet printer from computer images, and the results look great on light-colored muslin bags or cotton t-shirts. Folks wearing the t-shirts or carrying the bags can serve as walking billboards for your urban CSA wherever they go.

Public Relations

Communication is often described as a two-way street, and we have definitely found that we need our members to communicate with us as much as we need staff and team leaders to communicate with the membership at large to get work done, have volunteers when we need them, get relevant information to the people who need it, and determine how the CSA is succeeding.

But there is definitely a third element to communications—publicity comes into the equation, letting the world at large know about your urban CSA. This is essentially a way to market your CSA (covered in Chapter 3, Finding People to Join Your CSA), but keep in mind that this is another task of the communications committee. You should find one or two volunteers who can let the local press know when something of interest happens at the urban farm—maybe hiring a new farmer, or winning a beautification award, or simply the first harvest of the season.

A FINAL WORD

You will use communications to recruit members at the start of your CSA and in subsequent seasons, and then you must communicate with those members to get volunteers to help with the work and to have the CSA's activities run smoothly. Beyond that, you will communicate information about the CSA to rally support (and grants) from the public at large, announce events and honors involving your CSA, and educate the public about what you are doing with a local urban agriculture project.

It's important to make sure you *are* communicating, and remember that the words *community* and *communication* have the same root. Both come from the Latin *communicare,* which means "to share or make common." Share the information, share the work, and make common cause—and your CSA will thrive, both virtually and agriculturally. ■

Chapter 8

Beyond the Farm: CSA Odds and Ends

Practice yourself, in little things,
and then proceed to greater.
—*Epictetus*

W e have covered many aspects involved with starting an urban CSA in the previous chapters, but there are a few subjects that don't quite fit with any of the chapter topics. This final chapter includes information about a few additional topics that you may find useful as you start farming in the city. These topics include working cooperatively with other farms and retail outlets in your area, the pros and cons of organic certification, questions your members may have and CSA policies you should let them know about, and selecting and using CSA management software. The chapter ends with a look at how an urban CSA can be more than just a source of fresh, local, healthy food—it can also help your community become a better place to live, in both tangible and intangible ways.

WORKING WITH OTHER FARMS

There are two related reasons to work with other farms or farm markets: the first is to increase the variety of produce you have for members and the second is to find an outlet to sell or barter your surplus crops. Mixed markets—selling produce outside your CSA shares—can add stability and income to your urban farm, and many CSAs take advantage of other outlets to sell excess produce. First, however, let's talk about buying and selling or bartering with other farms to increase variety.

A transaction like this could be very simple—you have ten bushels of beans and you only need six bushels to give your members each a reasonable amount of beans in their share. The orchard on the outskirts of town has harvested its apples, but counts on other farms around the area to supply different produce for their farm stand. You can work out a deal to get a few bushels of apples in exchange for your excess green beans, and everyone is happy.

There are a thousand permutations to this scenario—bartering, even trades, selling in weeks when you have excess and using the income to buy from other farms in weeks when you need to diversify or add to your own crops for the shares. You could set up a farm stand yourself to sell to customers outside your CSA base when you have more beans (or tomatoes or peppers) than members can use. Or you can enlist members to take the surplus to your local farmers' market and sell it there.

Having too much is a good problem, and one you should have at times since your farmer will probably grow a little more of most

Making connections with other farms and farmers in your area can help you set up a network to allow you to manage surpluses and deficits more efficiently (Photo: Nancy Sullivan)

items in order to guarantee enough for each pickup. Investigate the possibilities for selling your excess produce—seek out other growers near your location, scout farmers' markets, and try to determine the demand for fresh, locally grown produce outside your CSA members to see if it makes sense to forge some alliances or set up a network that will allow you to manage surpluses and deficits by working with other sellers and growers nearby.

One way to ensure that you have enough and a variety of produce for your CSA is to see if there are any nearby farms that might have fields that can be gleaned of food left in the fields. If the farmer is agreeable, CSA members or staff could arrange to go through the fields and gather this food for distribution at the next pickup.

There is another aspect of working with other farms—to offer your members items that you don't produce. The products could range from meat and dairy to fresh eggs, honey, and other items. You may want to offer some items as part of a regular share, provide them for people who are interested in ordering items in advance, or just having some products available for people to purchase when they come to pick up weekly shares.

Again, you are adding to the work of managing the CSA, but it could well be worth the added work if it keeps members coming back and helps make the project solvent. If you use CSA management software, you can set it up to allow members to buy extra items outside of the standard share, and this can make the process more manageable. It's probably a good idea to gauge interest from your members before embarking on an ambitious program of adding extra items for sale, but if the interest is there and the products are high quality and a good value, it's another way your CSA can retain members, by providing what they want. Remember to add a little to the cost you pay for the items to cover the expenses involved in procuring and providing the items and to cover any that are not purchased; you don't want to lose money by offering these items to members.

If your CSA grows more than you need for member shares, you could set up a farmstand to sell directly to the public or talk to restaurants and other retail outlets about supplying them with fresh produce

SELLING AT OTHER OUTLETS

Mixing markets adds a level of complexity to your operation. You have to decide if the potential income that comes from selling at other outlets is worth that added complexity. Many things will enter into the decision, including the availability of farmers' markets or wholesale outlets for what you have to sell. You also have to consider your members—especially if you are a co-operative farm, keeping the members satisfied with what they receive in their shares and in return for their work at the farm is the most important objective.

But if you find there is a demand for something you can grow, it's a way to increase income and keep your share prices reasonable. We have found local restaurants who were interested in purchasing surplus produce when we have a bumper crop of an item. We've also talked to chefs about supplying locally grown items that we might not necessarily grow for members but which we could make room for as a cash crop. An example is a Vietnamese restaurant that was looking for a local source of cilantro and lemongrass; growing these herbs in a small amount of space and providing them to the restaurant regularly could provide extra income and help balance the books.

Some possibilities for other markets for produce include both retail, such as an on-site farm stand, a vegetable wagon that travels around the neighborhood, or a nearby farmers' market; and wholesale, including food co-ops, other CSAs, chefs/restaurants, and schools or institutions. There are logistics involved beyond actually growing the crops: you will need people available to staff the farm stand, vegetable wagon, or farmers' market booth; for wholesale, this would also entail invoicing, collecting, and delivering the products.

Selling to other markets is an opportunity to expand your sales and increase your income, but you need to balance that with the added work to decide if this is right for your urban farm.

ORGANIC CERTIFICATION

Most CSAs, including the Enright Ridge CSA, use organic methods to grow their crops. However, we are not certified organic, and there are many other CSAs out there that grow organically without official certification. The main reason why many CSA farms are not certified organic is that it is an expensive and time-consuming process. If you grow at multiple locations, it could become unreasonably costly to have every garden or field certified organic.

The term "organic" is now legally defined and can be used only when describing produce grown in accordance with USDA rules and certified organic by an independent certification agency. Do you need to have your urban CSA certified organic? Maybe not—if your members know and trust the farmer, and work on the crops themselves, they will probably be satisfied that organic practices are being used. But don't call your farm "organic" in advertising or promotions if it is not certified.

There are reasons to get certified, especially if you plan to sell your produce to other markets. If you sell at a farmers' market, you may command a higher price for items that are certified organic. And if you plan to sell to restaurants or other retail outlets, they may demand certified organic products.

POLICY STATEMENT

You need a written document that sets out the policies established for your CSA regarding payment, pickup, work, and any other aspects of the urban farm that need to be clearly set out. A co-operative CSA is an agreement among members and the farm staff to do what is required of them, in a timely fashion, according to some established expectations. Some things you want to cover in your policy statement include the following statements, revised as necessary to reflect the specific situations of your CSA:

1. I understand that I am supporting local food production and sharing in the harvest.

2. I understand and accept the risks involved with agriculture and how this can affect the yield and variety of produce in shares, and I agree to share in the bounty and loss of the season.

3. I agree to make payment for my share on time and in full as scheduled.

4. I understand that there are no refunds after the first pickup of the season.

5. I agree to fulfill the farm work hour commitment I have made by selecting a specific type of share, and I understand that I am responsible for keeping track of the hours I work.

6. I understand that I am responsible for taking care of CSA tools used in performing work, returning them when finished.

7. I agree to keep my membership contact information up to date.

8. I agree that it is my responsibility to pick up my weekly distribution of produce at the designated site and time.

9. I understand that if I am unable to pick up my CSA share during a vacation or for any other reason, I must make arrangements for someone else to pick it up or let the packout team know I will not be getting a share that week.

10. I agree to read all communications from the farm.

You may want to include more information about payments, and you will probably have other items to add to your policy statement, but this gives you a good outline to get started.

FREQUENTLY ASKED QUESTIONS

There are certain things that new or potential members need to know about the CSA, and you will find that many of the same questions come up again and again. It's worth your while to construct a list of frequently asked questions and answers to provide to people. This can be a short list in your promotional brochure or a longer list on your website. Following are a few of the questions we are often asked, with answers to each one.

What is a CSA?

CSA is an abbreviation for "Community Supported Agriculture." Most CSAs are created by forming a contract between a farmer and a group of people who pay in advance for the crops he or she grows, sharing the risk and the bounty. All members of the CSA pay for their shares and/or commit to a certain number of work hours.

What do I owe for my share, and how do I make a payment?

Check the website to see a list of the costs of different size shares with different work hour amounts. We ask for a deposit with your application, so if you have paid your deposit, subtract that from the amount for the share you have selected and either mail a check for the balance, or bring it to the greenhouse during packout.

Where and when do we get produce?

The Enright Ridge CSA provides produce to members for six months of the year, from May through October. Shares are distributed every Saturday morning during growing season and can be picked up at the distribution location.

How do I know what we'll be getting in the weekly share?

We post a newsletter every week with what we think will be ready for distribution on Saturday, but these items can change. The packout team also labels the items for pickup, so you can make a list while you are at the greenhouse if you are unfamiliar with any of the produce.

What happens if I forget to pick up my share?

If you forget to pick up your share and haven't contacted the packout team to pack it up for later pickup, well, you just don't get a share that week. Since we are a co-op with limited personnel, it isn't possible to have people available for share distribution outside of regular hours.

What if I can't make it to the greenhouse on Saturday morning?

We can accommodate you if you let the packout leader know in advance that you'd like to pick up your share later. We'll pack up your share and leave it in the cooler with your name on it. This is a service we provide as needed, but please don't abuse the privilege. If you can never pick up on time and cannot make arrangements for someone else to pick up your share for you, perhaps this CSA is not a good choice for you.

Enright Ridge CSA currently uses a CSA management software program called Farmigo to provide online signup and payment by credit card for our members

CSA MANAGEMENT SOFTWARE

Our urban CSA managed for several years using various computerized elements, such as Google Docs, Excel, and QuickBooks, to keep track of the business of farming. It served us well, but we were also intrigued by the notion of having a software management system that provided all the accounting and member management elements we needed in one package. So we started looking at CSA management software.

If you search online for that phrase, you will find that there are several choices, and one thing that they have in common is that they are generally set up for what we'll call a classic community supported agriculture business—a farmer who is growing and selling for profit and who is using the CSA model to ensure that he or she has a market for his crops in advance.

This is not how our urban CSA is set up. One major drawback of commonly available CSA software is that it does not address having members who work at the farm as well as pay for a share of the produce. The management software also offers more features than a small urban CSA may need, but if you can justify the monthly cost (most providers charge a percentage of your sales, which in the case of a co-op CSA farm is the amount charged for your shares divided by the number of months you provide produce) then you should look into what these programs offer and how they can streamline your operations.

ESTABLISHING VALUE CHAINS WITH YOUR CSA

A value chain is a chain of activities performed on raw materials to create something more valuable (a product or service) than the sum of the cost of the raw materials. When you are working to establish an urban CSA, it is helpful to consider how the resources invested in urban farming can bring more value than the price paid for them.

There is a temptation for people to go to the supermarket and buy their fruits and vegetables there because they are cheap. Stores use fresh fruits and vegetables as loss leaders to get people in the door. They are willing to lose some money on produce because their real profit is in processed foods. It is hard to convince people in our society to pay a little extra for an item even if it is clearly of higher quality; we are always looking for bargains and ways to "save." It is difficult, when pricing shares, to find the point at which you can farm productively but stay competitive with the supermarkets.

The value added in produce from a garden involves the work of the community. It's possible to see an increase in value of up to six times the cost of seeds and water in what the harvested vegetables were worth. Of course, there are many more expenses involved in running a CSA than just seeds and water, but in the long run, the resources invested in urban farming can bring more value than the price paid.

Some things of value that the CSA provides:

Shareholders and their families, interns, and students in the community benefit from the establishment of a CSA when they learn more about where their food comes from (PHOTO: NANCY SULLIVAN)

▶ Training for interns who can go on to find another position in farming, increasing the number of local, sustainable urban farms

▶ Locally grown organic food that lowers our carbon footprint

▶ Truly fresh fruits and vegetables that provide greater nutrition

All of this raises the value of the food we get at the CSA—and we receive a lot more than just a bag of vegetables once a week:

▶ Shareholders get the opportunity to learn about gardening.

▶ They can see the fields where their food is grown and how it is grown.

▶ They join with other people who value quality food to form a supportive community.

▶ They can share recipes and ideas about preparing fresh, wholesome food.

LABOR ISSUES

Like any business, the CSA needs to be aware of issues involving its labor force, both paid and unpaid. Liability insurance is important in case someone gets hurt doing farm work or just visiting the premises. There are also a lot of other aspects of having employees, including regulations regarding the minimum wage, workers' comp coverage, tax withholding, and other requirements of labor law.

Tasks such as watering nursery starts can be done by CSA volunteers and workshare members with a minimum of training and supervision

There are ways to avoid having to get too involved with labor law, including hiring staff on a contract, so that they are essentially self-employed, doing the farm work for you according to a contract you negotiate in advance rather than as a salaried or hourly employee. Although this is an option, and one we have used, the argument can be made that it shortchanges the farmer. We want to see urban farms in every neighborhood, as a sustainable way to provide food and work for people in cities. In the long run, we have a goal of making sure urban farm workers are paid a living wage and reasonable benefits to make this work rewarding in every way.

For now, however, we want the urban farm model to become established, and in some cases that means negotiating a compromise to make it possible to pay the farm staff. The Vista and AmeriCorps programs are another way we have found to acquire lower-cost employees, and in those cases, most of the paperwork and tax requirements are taken care of by the umbrella organization providing the workers rather than being the responsibility of the CSA. We want to believe that someday urban farms will be a common source of employment for skilled people in our cities, but for now, we need to find creative ways to compensate workers properly, and this can include anything from on-the-job training to help with housing in addition to a salary.

Interns and Trainees

You may have some staff members who are learning how to farm and are willing to work either as unpaid trainees or as interns at a fairly low wage in return for the training they receive. This provides benefits on both sides, because your CSA gets hard-working staff and the trainees get a unique chance to learn while doing. Although some people are uncomfortable with this arrangement, feeling it can take advantage of the interns and trainees, keep in mind that many people pay large sums of money to attend colleges and vocational schools to learn a profession or trade, and even people working in their chosen fields often pay to attend workshops or acquire continuing education credits to keep up to date with the methods used for their work.

We believe that the hands-on experience we can give interns and trainees is a superior way to learn to farm, and it is an comparatively inexpensive way to learn a useful and valuable trade. These staff members still may be considered employees from a legal standpoint, however. Check with your local laws, and make sure you and your intern/trainees both understand up front what is involved in the training program you provide insofar as wages and other benefits are concerned.

Work Share Workers

Many CSAs require working hours for their members, and if you set up as a co-operative farm, you will definitely depend on your members to do much of the work on the farm. With minimal training and proper supervision, shareholders can help with planting, watering, pest management, harvest, and many other chores, both on the farm side and the business side.

That's one of the reasons members join a co-op CSA, to make a real connection with growing their own food. They want to get their hands dirty and get involved with the work, and many tasks are available without too much training. It also makes sense to find out if members have any skills they can apply to jobs around the farm, from accounting to sign painting to tool repair.

JOB CREATION

As family farms have disappeared, there are fewer opportunities for people who love farming to find a way to pursue this as an occupation. An urban CSA provides employment for farmers, and it also allows others who are interested to learn to farm as interns. But that's not the only way it can have an impact on employment in the community. A CSA may choose to purchase eggs from a neighbor, buy tools and have them sharpened at the local hardware store, or find a source of locally grown seeds. All of these, while not providing jobs directly, can provide people in the area with an outlet for their goods and can help make their jobs and their businesses profitable.

In the long run, an urban CSA may decide to provide food products for sale with added value. If you have access to a commercial kitchen, you may even consider processing some of what you grow to sell as packaged foods. The possibilities are perhaps not endless, but with a little creative thinking, there are ways to make local food production a source of employment for people in the neighborhood.

Strengthening the Community

It's been said that gardens and farms in city neighborhoods can help create a sense of place. Whether you actively seek to con-

Urban farms and gardens can create a sense of community and help bring together diverse populations in city neighborhoods

struct a community around your farm or watch it develop on its own, you will find that the CSA you start will make people come together and create a stronger neighborhood spirit. Some CSAs attempt to be more inclusive by donating a few shares to families who otherwise would not be able to afford to be part of the farm. The goal is to support the community—and to watch as the community supports the farm, too.

We hope you will also benefit from the lessons we've learned at the Enright Ridge CSA, and we wish you success as you start your own urban farm project. You're helping us see our dream of having an urban CSA in every neighborhood, growing wholesome food together as a community. ■

References and Organizations

If you have a garden and a library,
you have everything you need.
—*Marcus Tullius Cicero*

REFERENCES

The following list includes articles and reports, books, periodicals, videos, and websites where you can find more information or just be inspired by how other people have accomplished successful farming ventures. It is by no means an exhaustive list, and we encourage you to investigate what else has been written on the challenges and accomplishments of urban farmers and community supported agriculture in your area and across the country. These resources can get you started.

Articles and Reports

City of Cincinnati. 2009. Urban Garden Policy Board Annual Report. http://city-egov.cincinnati-oh.gov/Webtop/ws/council/public/child/Blob/28900.pdf?rpp=-10&m=1&w=doc_no%3D%27200901532%27

CUESA. How Far Does Food Travel to Get to Your Plate? Cultivating a Healthy Food System. http://www.cuesa.org/page/how-far-does-your-food-travel-get-your-plate

Graff, Vincent. 10 December 2011. Carrots in the Car Park. Radishes on the Roundabout. The Deliciously Eccentric Story of the Town Growing ALL Its Own Veg. *The Daily Mail.* http://www.dailymail.co.uk/femail/article-2072383/Eccentric-town-Todmorden-growing-ALL-veg.html

Guide to Minimize Microbial Food Safety Hazards for Fresh Fruits and Vegetables. http://www.fda.gov/downloads/Food/GuidanceComplianceRegulatoryInformation/GuidanceDocuments/ProduceandPlanProducts/UCM169112.pdf

Hale, Jack. Insurance for Community Gardens. http://communitygarden.org/docs/learn/articles/insuranceforcommunitygardens.pdf

Hotchkiss, Julie. July 2008. Downtown on the Farm. *CityBeat.* http://www.citybeat.com/cincinnati/article-18305-downtown_on_the_farm.html

Kaufman, Jerry, and Martin Bailkey. 2009. Farming Inside Cities: Entrepreneurial Urban Agriculture in the United States. http://www.urbantilth.org/wp-content/uploads/2008/10/farminginsidecities.pdf

Voicu, Ioan, and Vicki Been. The Effect of Community Gardens on Neighboring Property Values. http://onlinelibrary.wiley.com/doi/10.1111/j.1540-6229.2008.00213.x/abstract

Books

Allen, Will. 2012. *The Good Food Revolution.* New York: Gotham Books.

Carpenter, Novella. 2010. *Farm City: The Education of an Urban Farmer.* New York: Penguin Books.

Carpenter, Novella, and Willow Rosenthal. 2011. *The Essential Urban Farmer.* New York: Penguin Books.

Hayes, Shannon. 2010. *Radical Homemakers: Reclaiming Domesticity from a Consumer Culture,* Left to Write Press.

Logsdon, Gene. 2010. *Holy Shit: Managing Manure to Save Mankind.* White River Junction, VT: Chelsea Green Publishing.

Rich, Sarah S. 2012. *Urban Farms.* New York: Harry Abrams.

Periodicals

Acres U.S.A.—A Voice for Eco-Agriculture, monthly magazine.

American Small Farmer, monthly farm magazine.

Growing for Market, trade publication for local food growers; covers farmers' markets, CSAs, the local food movement, organic growing, and more.

The Leopold Letter, quarterly newsletter from the Leopold Center for Sustainable Agriculture.

Mother Earth News, bimonthly magazine with information about sustainable living.

The Natural Farmer, Quarterly newspaper from the Northeast Organic Farming Association.

Urban Agriculture Magazine, a publication of the RUAF Foundation (Resource Centre for Urban Agriculture & Food Security).

Videos

Community Supported Agriculture: What to Expect When You Join a Farm. Available on YouTube at http://www.youtube.com/watch?v=H-e7asz-XE0

The Real Dirt on Farmer John, 2005. Documentary film. Angelic Organics, Taggart Siegel, director. Chronicles the resurrection of a family farm in Illinois through its conversion to a CSA model. http://www.angelicorganics.com/ao/index.php?option=com_content&task=view&id=148&Itemid=182

Urban Roots, 2011. Documentary film. Tree Media, Mark MacInnis, director. Tells the story of the spontaneous emergence of urban farming in Detroit. http://treemedia.com/treemedia.com/Urban_Roots.html

The American Planning Association Guidelines for Sustainable City Growth: http://www.planning.org/research/index.htm#completed

The Beginning Farmer: http://www.beginningfarmers.org

Campbell River Community Farm Multi Phase Action Plan: http://communityfarmproject.wordpress.com/project-proposal-4/

Community Supported Agriculture in Michigan: http://CSAFarms.org

The Contrary Farmer (Gene Logsdon): http://thecontraryfarmer.wordpress.com

The Edible Schoolyard Project (Alice Walters School Lunch Initiative): http://edibleschoolyard.org

Enright Ridge Community Supported Agriculture Project: http://www.enright-csa.org

Farmers' Guide to Securing Land, California FarmLink: http://www.californiafarmlink.org

Farmer's Markets: Guide to Setting Up a Stand and Marketing Produce Post-Harvest: http://www.ams.usda.gov/AMSv1.0/ams.fetchTemplateData.do?template=TemplateN&navID=WholesaleandFarmersMarkets&leftNav=WholesaleandFarmersMarkets&page=WFMFarmersMarketsandDirecttoConsumerMarketing&description=Farmers%20Markets%20and%20Direct%20to%20Consumer%20Marketing&acct=frmrdirmkt

Field Guide for Beginning Farmers: http://fieldguideforbeginningfarmers.wikispaces.com/

Harmonious Homestead, Rachel Tayse Baillieul's blog about suburban farming near Columbus, Ohio: http://www.harmonioushomestead.com

Irrigation Energy Estimator: http://ipat.sc.egov.usda.gov/

Organic Consumer's Association Resource Center on Farm Issues, organic science news, action alerts, and links to other groups: http://www.organicconsumers.org

The Ohio State University Department of Horticulture and Crop Science, Good Agricultural Practices (GAP) Fruit and Vegetable Safety Program: http://producesafety.osu.edu/gaps

SARE (Sustainable Agriculture Research & Education) offers competitive grants for researchers, agricultural educators, students, farmers, ranchers, and youth in the United States: http://www.sare.org/Grants/Grants-Information

Soil Assessment: http://www.soils.wisc.edu/foe/login

Soil Association: http://www.soilassociation.org/Takeaction/Getinvolvedlocally/Communitysupportedagriculture/tabid/201/Default.aspx

Tool for comparing nutrient value and cost of cover crops, fertilizers, and compost: http://smallfarms.oregonstate.edu/calculator

Urban Agriculture News Service: http://urbanagriculture-news.com/

Urban Tilth, provides a solid reference section with abstracts for the links: http://www.urbantilth.org/resources/policies-programs-initiatives-and-information-to-help-grow-urban-foodsheds/

USDA Good Agricultural Practices Audit Programs: http://www.ams.usda.gov/AMSv1.0/HarmonizedGAP

Vancouver City Farmer News: http://www.cityfarmer.info/about/

ORGANIZATIONS

There are plenty of organizations that can help you learn to farm in the city. Make connections with some of the people who have gone before you and you can benefit from what they've tried and found to work—as well as what doesn't work. Meetings and conferences are also a chance to be inspired by how many people are growing their own food, in urban farms and rural settings, for farm markets and for community supported agriculture projects. You are not alone!

American Community Garden Association (ACGA): http://communitygarden.org

ATTRA, National Sustainable Agriculture Information Service: https://attra.ncat.org/calendar/index.php

Central Ohio River Valley Food Guide: http://www.eatlocalcorv.org

Civic Garden Center of Greater Cincinnati Community Gardens Program: http://www.civicgardencenter.org/garden_files/NG.htm

Closing the Health Gap Food Access Initiative, Dwight Tillery, CEO: http://www.closingthehealthgap.org/What/Initiatives.html

Enright Ridge Urban EcoVillage: http://www.enrightecovillage.org

Growing Power, Will Allen's organization, based in Milwaukee: http://www.growingpower.org

Hamilton County Soil & Water Conservation District: http://www.hcswcd.org

Ohio Ecological Food and Farm Association: http://www.oeffa.org

The Land Institute, Wes Jackson's organization for the study of natural systems and permaculture: http://www.landinstitute.org/

Appendix A

Useful Forms for Planning for an Urban CSA

This appendix includes copies of forms and guides that can help you plan for your urban CSA. There are planting guides, sample budgets, team lists, and other planning tools that we have found or developed at the Enright Ridge CSA. You will develop your own forms and guides as your urban farm gets underway, but these will help you get started.

▶ Planting Guides (CSAFarms.org, Michigan Community Supported Agriculture)

▶ Crop Planting Chart (CSAFarms.org, Michigan Community Supported Agriculture)

▶ Useful Planting Information (CSAFarms.org, Michigan Community Supported Agriculture)

▶ Sample CSA Budget (Enright Ridge CSA)

▶ Sample CSA Work Hours Tracking Form (Enright Ridge CSA)

▶ Farmer Interview Questions (Enright Ridge CSA)

▶ Sample CSA Application (Enright Ridge CSA)

Crop	Planting Distance in Feet or Inches		Approximate yield per 10 feet of row	Approximate no. of row feet to plant per person	Transplants or seed per 10 feet of row	
	In Rows	Between Rows			No. of Plants	Amt of Seed
Asparagus	18"	48-60"	3-4 lbs.	15-20'	7-8 crowns	
Beans, bush	1-2"	24-30"	3-5 lbs.	20-50'		1 oz.
Beans, pole	4-12"	36-48"	6-10 lbs.	10-30'		1 oz.
Beans, lima	3-4"	24-36"	3-5 lbs.	20-30'		1 oz.
Beans, wax	2"	24-36"	3-5 lbs.	20-50'		1/8 oz.
Beets	2-3"	12-24"	8-10 lbs.	10'		1/8 oz.
Broccoli	15-24"	24-36"	4-6 lbs.	10-20'	5-8 or	1/10 oz.
Brussels Sprouts	18-24"	30-36"	3-4 lbs.	10'	5-7 or	1/10 oz.
Cabbage	15-18"	30-36"	10-25 lbs.	10-15'	5-8 or	1/10 oz.
Chinese Cabbage	12-24"	18-30"	20-30 lbs.	10-15'	8-12 or	1/5 oz.
Carrots	1-2"	15-30"	7-10 lbs.	10-20'		1/5 oz.
Cauliflower	14-24"	24-36"	8-10 lbs.	10-15'	5-8 or	1/10 oz.
Chard, Swiss	6-12"	18-30"	8-12 lbs.	5-10'		1/5 oz.
Collards	18-24"	24-36"	8-15 lbs.	10-15'	5-7 or	1/10 oz.
Cucumbers	12-18"	48-72"	8-10 lbs.	15-20'		1/10 oz.
Eggplant	18-24"	30-42"	10-12 lbs.	3-6'	5-7 or	1/40 oz.
Endive	9-12"	18-30"	3-6 lbs.	5-10'	5-10 or	1/40 oz.
Kale	10-18"	18-36"	4-8 lbs.	10-15'	6-10 or	1/10 oz.
Kohlrabi	4-6"	12-36"	4-8 lbs.	5-10'		1/10 oz.

Crop	Planting Distance		Approximate yield per 10 feet of row	Approximate no. of row feet to plant per person	Transplants or seed per 10 feet of row		
	In Rows	Between Rows				No. of Plants	Amt of Seed
Leeks	3-6"	12-30"	10-20 lbs.	3-6'			1/10 oz.
Lettuce (Bibb)	6-10"	14-24"	4-8 lbs.	15-20'			1/40 oz.
Lettuce (leaf)	4-6"	12-18"	5-10 lbs.	10-15'			1/40 oz.
Muskmelons	24-36"	60-90"	15-25 lbs.	8-12'		3-5 or	1/8 oz.
Mustard	3-4"	18-30"	3-6 lbs.	5-10'			1/10 oz.
Okra	12-18"	36-48"	5-10 lbs.	5-10'		7-10 or	1/5 oz.
Onions (sets)	2-4"	12-24"	7-10 lbs.	15-25'		30-60	1 lb.
Peas (English)	1-3"	12-30"	2-6 lbs.	40-60'			1/2 oz.
Peppers	18-24"	30-36"	5-18 lbs.	5-10'		5-7	NA
Potatoes, Irish	10-21"	24-36"	10-20 lbs.	75-100'			1 lb.
Pumpkins	4-7'	6-8'	10-20 lbs.	10'			1/20 oz.
Rutabaga	3-6"	15-30"	8-12 lbs.	5-10'			1/8 oz.
Southern Peas	2-4"	24-30"	5-18 lbs.	25-30'			1 oz.
Sweet Corn	9-12"	24-36"	7-10 lbs.	40-60'			1/2 oz.
Spinach	3-6"	15-30"	4-6 lbs.	30-40'			1/8 oz.
Squash, summer	24-36"	36-60"	20-80 lbs.	5-10'			1/10 oz.
Squash, winter	3-7'	3-10'	10-80 lbs.	10'			1/10 oz.
Sweet Potatoes	12-18"	36-48"	8-12 lbs.	75-100'		7-10	NA
Tomatoes	18-36"	36"	15-45 lbs.	10-15'		3-7	NA
Turnips	2-3"	12-24"	8-12 lbs.	10'			1/8 oz.
Watermelons	6-8'	7-10'	8-40 lbs.	10-15'		1-2	1/2 oz.

Crop	# wks	Amount/ wk	unit	Total Amount/ yr	Yield/ bed-ft	bed-ft needed
Arugula, early	3	0.5	lb	15	4.5	3
Beans, bush 1	2	1	lb	20	1.2	17
Beans, bush 2	2	1	lb	20	1.2	17
Beets, late/storage	12	2	lb	240	3	80
Br. sprouts	6	2	lb	120	1.2	100
Broccoli, early	10	1	hd	100	1.34	75
Broccoli, late	10	1	hd	100	1.34	75
Cabb, early	3	1	hd	30	1.34	22
Cabb, late	10	1	hd	100	1.34	75
Carrots, early	10	2	lb	200	4.5	44
Carrots, late/storage	29	2.25	lb	652.5	4.5	145
Cauliflower, late	6	1	hd	60	1.005	60
Chard, early	8	2	lb	160	0.75	75
Chard, late *cut for salad first	8	2	lb	160	0.75	100
Chin Cabb, early	2	1	hd	20	1.005	20
Corn, sweet 1 (2 var)	2	12	ea	240	1.95	123
Corn, sweet 2 (2 var)	2	12	ea	240	1.5	160
Cucumber, early	4	2	lb	80	0.9	300
Cucumber, mid	4	2	lb	80	0.9	300
Eggplant	8	1	lb	80	1	80
Kale, early	8	2	lb	160	1.125	142
Kohlrabi, late	4	3	ea	120	4.5	27
Leeks	19	2	ea	380	6	63
Lettuce, early	6	2	hd	120	3	40
Lettuce, late	8	2	hd	160	4.5	36
Melons, late	6	1	ea	60	0.75	80
Onion, storage	33	3	ea	990	6	165
Peas	4	0.5	lb	20	0.15	133
Peppers, sweet	10	2	lb	200	0.75	360
Peppers, hot	6	0.25	lb	15	0.375	100
Potato	25	2.25		562.5	1.5	375
Radish, Daikon	4	1	lb	40	2.25	18
Radish, early	6	1	bu	60	4.5	13
Radish, late	6	1	bu	60	4.5	13
Spinach, early	4	1	lb	40	1.2	33
Squash, sum, early	3	1.6	lb	48	1.5	32
Squash, sum, mid	3	1.6	lb	48	1.5	32
Squash, sum, late	3	1.6	lb	48	1.5	32
Squash, win, grp3 B-Nut, Acorn	8	5	lb	400	1.5	267
Squash, win, grp4 Delicata	3	5	lb	150	1.5	100
Tomato, main	10	4	lb	400	1.125	680

Variety - Type	Planting Rate Seed Needed		Estimate # of seeds per oz	Planting Distance		Depth to plant inches	Time to mature Days
CLICK NAME FOR MORE INFO	100' Row	Acre		In Rows	Space Rows		
Beans, Pole	1/2-1 lbs.	30-40 lbs.	60-100	3-8"	36-48"	1-1.5	50-70
Beans, Snap	1-2 lbs.	60-100 lbs.	100	1-4"	18-40"	1-1.5	40-60
Beans Bush Lima	1-2 lbs.	30-50 lbs.	25-60	6-8"	18-30"	1-1.5	40-65
Beets, Mono-germ	1-1.5 oz.	5-10 lbs.	800-1000	1-2"	18-24"	1/2	55-75
Beets, Multi-germ	2 oz.	8-24 lbs.	1,500	1-4"	18-24"	1/2	58-80
Broccoli*	1/2 oz.	1/4 lb.	9,000	18-24"	2-3'	1/4	100-130
Brussels Sprouts	1/2 oz.	1/4 lb.	8,000	18-24"	24-30"	1/4	150
Cabbage*	1/2 oz.	1/4 lb.	8,500	8-30"	2-3'	1/4	65-120
Cabbage**	1/2 oz.	1-3 lbs.	8,500	8-30"	2-3'	1/4	75-120
Cabbage, Chinese	1/2 oz.	3-4 lbs.	17,000	12-18"	2-3'	1/4	79-80
Carrot	1/2 oz.	2-5 lbs.	25,000	1-3"	18-24"	1/2	100-120
Cauliflower	1/4 oz.	1/4 lb.	10,000	18-24"	2-3'	1/4	120-150
Collards	1/2 oz.	3-4 lbs.	8,000	4-8"	18-24"	1/4	60-80
Celery***	1/4 oz.	1/4 lb.	60,000	6"	2-3'	1/8	100-130
Cucumber	1 oz.	3 lbs.	1000	1-3'	3-6'	1	60-90
Egg Plant ***	1/4 oz.	1/4 lb.	6,000	18-24"	2-3'	1/2	120-130
Endive	1 oz.	4 lbs.	25,000	8-12"	18-24"	1/2	85-100
Kale	1/2 oz.	4 lbs.	7,500	12-24"	18-24"	1/2	50-60
Kohl Rabi	1/2 oz.	4 lbs.	8,000	6-8"	18-24"	1/2	50-60
Lettuce	1/4 oz.	3-4 lbs.	25,000	6-12"	18-24"	1/8	60-90
Musk Melons	1 oz.	3 lbs.	1200	3-4"	6-8"	1	85-100
Mustard	1 oz.	5 lbs.	15,000	4-6"	6-8'	1/4	50-70
Okra	2 oz.	8 lbs.	500	18-24"	2-3'	1	50-60
Onions, Green	1 oz.	3-4 lbs.	8,000	2-3'	15-30"	1/2	60-90
Onions, Dry	1 oz.	3-4 lbs.	8,000	2-3"	15-30"	1/2	140-180
Parsley	3/4 oz.	4 lbs.	15,000	4-8"	12-18"	1/4	90
Parsnip	1 oz.	4 lbs.	10,000	3-6"	18-24"	3/4	120
Peas (Rows)	2 lbs.	90-150 lbs.	90-150	2-3"	2-3'	1.5-2	60-120
Peas (Broadcast)	---	200-250 lb.	90-150	---	---	1.5-2	60-120
Pepper ***	1/8 oz.	6 oz.	4,000	15-20"	18-30"	1/4	75-120
Pepper **	1/2 lb.	2 lbs.	4,000	15-20"	18-30"	1/4	75-120
Pumpkin	1 oz.	3 lbs.	4,000	15-20"	18-30"	1/4	75-120
Radish	1 oz.	10-12 lbs.	2,500	.5-1"	12-18"	1/2	28-36
Rutabaga	1/2 oz.	2-4 lbs.	10,000	6-8"	18-24"	1/2	70-100
Spinach	1 oz.	10-15 lbs.	2,500	3-4"	12-18"	1/2-3/4	40-65
Squash, Summer	2 oz.	4-6 lbs.	300	3-4'	3-4'	1&1/2	60-75
Squash, Winter	1 oz.	3-4 lbs.	100	4-6'	6-8'	1&1/2	75-100
Sweet Corn	1/2 oz.	1.5-2 lbs.	11,000	1.5-6'	3-7'	1/4	60-90
Tomato **	1/4 oz.	1/4 lb.	11,000	2-4'	3-4'	1/4	60-90
Tomato ***	1/4 oz.	1/4 lb.	11,000	2-4'	3-4'	1/4	60-90
Turnip	3/4 oz.	2 lbs.	10,000	3-4"	15-24"	1/4-1/2	45-60
Watermelon	1 oz.	2-4 lbs.	200-300	6-8'	8'	1-2	80-90

* = Usually started indoors in early spring and transplanted. Planting rate based on that method.
** = Columns 1 & 2 for planting rate based on direct seeding.
*** = Transplanted

Planting Notes: Seeding rates and spacing recommended above are, for the most part, figured on the basis of harvest by hand. High density planting rates and precision seed placement is now used on most mechanically harvested and grown vegetable crops. Different seeding rates would apply to those methods of propagation. The effect of arrangement and plant density in relation to fruit size, quality and total yield will vary depending on your local environmental conditions during the planting, growing and harvest seasons. Plant density must depend greatly on available planting and harvesting equipment. Seeding rates should depend in part on the total seed count (per oz/lb.) of seed in the particular lot being used, taking in to account the germination rate.

ERUEV – CSA (First Year of CSA)
FINANCIAL REPORT 2009

General Program	
Americorps and Vista	248.00
Farmers	6,022.26
Insurance	1,286.25
Total General Program	**7,556.51**
Greenhouse Program	
Utilities	674.20
Total Greenhouse Program	**674.20**
Local CSA Program	
Plants / Seeds / Supplies	1,368.89
Production Supplies / Tools	0.00
Products for Resale	25.00
Total Local CSA Program	**1,393.89**
Total Farm Project Operations	**9,624.60**
EXPENSES	
CSA Shares	**7,683.00**
Donations - General Support	**3,570.75**
Fundraising Sales	**180.50**
Total Farm Project	**11,434.25**

ENRIGHT RIDGE CSA WORK HOURS FORM 2013

Name

Date	Place	Activity	Hours	Total Hours

THE FARMER INTERVIEW PROCESS

In advance of the interview, ask the candidates to send you a resume and a cover letter. Also, ask for two business references and two personal references. Go through the resumes and pick out two to three farmers that most interest you. (If there is only one, or are more than three that seem competent, feel free to go with your inclinations.) When you select the people to interview, go back through their resumes and work out some questions you might have about each specific person based on their resumes.

Below are some other possible questions you might ask as a way to get to understand the people better. This is not a formula for interviewing. It is rather a list of ideas and questions that we would recommend you go through, selecting the ones that would best suit your CSA's circumstances, and add others that would be helpful. What we do recommend is that you have a set of questions going into the interview. It will make the interview flow more smoothly. You should always ask follow-up questions based on answers you may get during the interview as well. Be relaxed, enjoy the opportunity to interview a potential farmer, and you should have a good experience.

SOME QUESTIONS FOR FARMER CANDIDATES

- How did you hear about this position, and what attracted you to applying?

- What would you do the first month?

- What most excites you about this position?

- Why do you feel qualified for this position.

- What experience have you had in training and supervising farmers.

- Talk about your work with interns, with volunteers.

- What have you told your friends about this job.

- In light of what you know, what would be your vision for the Farm Project.

- Tell us about the best farming job you've ever had.

- Share an experience that's been pivotal to your personal development.

- How would your friends and co-workers describe you.

- Describe your ideal work environment.

- Why do you want to work for our CSA?

- What are you going to bring to work, relationships, and the future of the CSA?

As the interview proceeds, be sure to ask the interviewees if they have any questions of you. These questions will be important to them, but also to you, to see what they want to know.

(Continued)

(continued from previous page)

REFERENCES

We strongly recommend that you follow up on the references that people give you. Frequently you may not learn a lot from them, but other times checking references can be very informative.

When you talk to a candidate's references, first see if the candidate told them you were calling and if they know what the job is. If they don't, you might spend a little time explaining the position. Following are some questions that can provide you with background information about your farmer candidates:

- ▶ How do you know the candidate?

- ▶ What most impresses you about his/her farming skills?

- ▶ What do you think are his/her greatest strengths?

- ▶ What would you say are his/her possible weaknesses?

- ▶ Would you consider his/her for a job like this?

Enright Ridge Urban Eco-Village CSA 2013 Application

Contact Information

Name	
Street Address	
City ST ZIP Code	
Home Phone	
Cell Phone	
E-Mail Address	

Share Type

Share (Produce for 4+ people)

___ Non-work share: $750

___ Work share (40 hours): $550

Half Share (Produce for 2-3 people)

___ Non-work share: $425

___ Work share (20 hours) $325

You can pay for your share two ways: Pay in full with application, or use the installment plan, with one-third of the total due with application, one-third due by April 15th, and the balance (final one-third of total) due by May 15th. All shares must be paid in full by May 15th. (No refunds after first pickup)

Type of Work

There are several types of jobs that need to be fulfilled in order to keep the CSA running. They can be administrative (coordinating work shares, membership team, communications, social team, finance, and land development) as well as production work (plan team, propagation, nursery care, garden work, irrigation/watering, harvest and pack-out). You will have the opportunity at a member orientation to sign up for teams that suit your interests and availability.

Questions? Please check the FAQ page at our website or email urbanfarmproject@enright-csa.org

Return completed application with check for deposit made payable to ERUEV CSA. Send to:
ERUEV-CSA
PO Box 5206
Cincinnati, Ohio 45205

Office Use:
Check #_____ , Amount _____

- - - - - - - - - - - - TEAR OFF AND SAVE THIS RECEIPT FOR YOUR RECORDS - - - - - - - - - - - - -

ENRIGHT RIDGE 2013 CSA APPLICATION FOR _____

Check #_____ $_____ Deposit Date Paid _____

Appendix B

Using Social Media for CSA Communications

Chapter 7 covers the basics of creating a website and a blog for your CSA, but there's a lot more you can do online to stay connected to your current members and promote what you are doing to prospective members and the community at large. There are so many different ways to use social media to promote a cause or an organization these days that it was overwhelming to include them in the chapter on communications, so instead we'll list a few here, with some suggestions on how you can use each one.

You've got a website and a blog set up for your CSA. You're all set, right? Well, let's say that's a good start, but there are literally dozens of other online sites that can help you recruit new members and communicate with the members you already have as well as the community at large. If you are interested in having more information online, look into Yelp and Google Places to put your urban CSA on the electronic map in your community. These sites also allow people to post reviews about your place.

There's a good chance that people who join your CSA will be familiar with social media outlets, and you can find volunteers who are willing to put in some of their work share hours sitting in front of a computer instead of pulling weeds or washing carrots. Keep in mind that you may need volunteers to do online promotional work year-round, not just during the growing season.

Find someone who'd like to set up a Pinterest "pinboard," sort of a virtual bulletin board, where recipes, photos, and other items of interest from your CSA can be posted. You can post photographs on Picasa or Flickr or PhotoBucket; you can set up a Google+ page (if you think it's ever going to catch on); you can post YouTube videos showing how to plant or transplant or harvest or distribute your produce. The possibilities are literally endless ... here are just a few of the ways we are using the Internet to communicate what we are doing at the Enright Ridge CSA.

Facebook

We had a Facebook page before we had a website, and some smaller urban CSAs—and those who would rather spend more time farming and less time online—might choose to operate with a Facebook page and a blog as their only online presence.

Set up an organizational Facebook page by going to Facebook.com; under the Sign Up button, click on Create a Page. You will see choices for the kind of page you want to create. Most urban CSAs would use

"Cause or community" or "Local business or place." Choose a type and fill out the information required, then click the "I agree to Facebook Pages terms." (It's always a good idea to click on the terms and read them first, before you agree.) Click the Get Started button, and the page will create itself after you have provided the basic information.

If you've done the setup work on the Facebook page and provided some personal information, you will be one of the administrators or managers of the page. Keep in mind that you do need to have a personal Facebook page as well to be an administrator; if you do not have one, Facebook will ask you to create one and will walk you through the steps for that, too. After you have the Facebook page set up, you can easily add other administrators or managers. The specific command names change from time to time on Facebook (and on other websites of this type), but look for an Edit Page button, and then select Admin Roles or something similar to open a dialog box that allows you to add administrators.

Administrators or managers can post things to your Facebook page under your CSA page name, but anyone who is interested can post on your Facebook page, so members can join the online community and comment on your CSA's posts or add their own posts—comments or recipes, questions, photos, videos, or links to other sites of interest.

We have not had any trouble with inappropriate posts (so far), but if you do have a problem, the administrators can delete unwanted posts and block specific users from posting on your page, too. Remember the interactive, intertwining nature of the Internet, too; put a link to your Facebook page on your website and your blog, and post links to your blog on Facebook to get members who look at your Facebook page regularly to visit your blog, too. It's all circular, but creating webs of information keeps everyone at the farm connected.

Administrators can share the task of maintaining, updating, and checking up on your CSA's Facebook page. This is something that really needs to be attended to almost daily; post something about the week's produce, a cartoon that is on topic, or a link to an article or recipe, just to get people talking—so to speak—online. Figure on 10 to 15 minutes a day to keep your Facebook page current and useful to your online community. CSA members will pitch in with posts of their own to keep the page active, relevant, and up to date.

Twitter

Like Facebook, Twitter has become common. It's not all the latest celebrity gossip; for your CSA, it does have its practical uses, too. Twitter has the capability to be used by any team leader at your farm who needs help—it is very simple to use, messages are short (140 characters or less), and with an account name and password, anyone can post a call for workers from a computer or smartphone.

Now, the catch is that if you simply post something to Twitter, only people who also have Twitter accounts and have signed up to follow you on Twitter will get the message. However, it is easy to add a little code to a website page to create a Twitter feed, as they call it, which will post any Twitter messages from your account onto a website. We put ours on the Work page of our website, and we encourage team leaders to post work opportunities and members to check the Work page when they have time and want to do some work at the farm.

If you were scared off by that reference to code, don't worry. The ability to put a Twitter feed on your website is handled by a "widget" that does all the work for you; you just cut and paste the widget code into your website. Search for *Twitter widget* online, you will find links to the code you need and step-by-step directions on how to embed it in your website page.

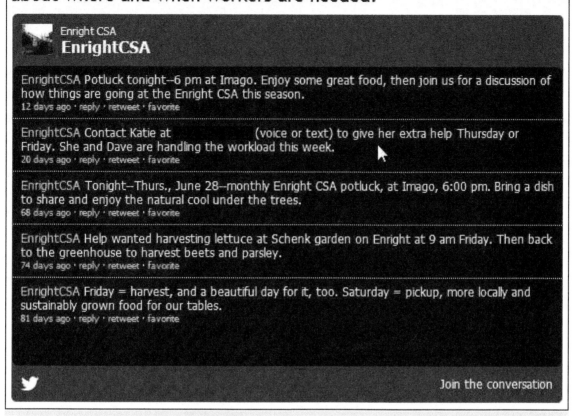

This season, we're using Twitter to post work opportunities as they come up. Follow us @EnrightCSA or check below for posts about where and when workers are needed.

Enright CSA
EnrightCSA

EnrightCSA Potluck tonight--6 pm at Imago. Enjoy some great food, then join us for a discussion of how things are going at the Enright CSA this season.
12 days ago · reply · retweet · favorite

EnrightCSA Contact Katie at   (voice or text) to give her extra help Thursday or Friday. She and Dave are handling the workload this week.
20 days ago · reply · retweet · favorite

EnrightCSA Tonight--Thurs., June 28--monthly Enright CSA potluck, at Imago, 6:00 pm. Bring a dish to share and enjoy the natural cool under the trees.
68 days ago · reply · retweet · favorite

EnrightCSA Help wanted harvesting lettuce at Schenk garden on Enright at 9 am Friday. Then back to the greenhouse to harvest beets and parsley.
74 days ago · reply · retweet · favorite

EnrightCSA Friday = harvest, and a beautiful day for it, too. Saturday = pickup, more locally and sustainably grown food for our tables.
81 days ago · reply · retweet · favorite

Join the conversation

You can create a Twitter feed on your website Work page so that anyone who checks the site can see if work opportunities have been posted

And if this still sounds too complicated, let us reassure you with two thoughts—first, we didn't know what we were doing when we started putting together our website. We learned on the fly, looking things up as needed, and it only hurt our heads a little bit. Now we have a little knowledge—a dangerous thing—and still manage to stay just a step or two ahead of what we need to keep all of our online balls in the air. But we do manage it!

Second, if you just can't handle the idea of trying to figure it out on your own, enlist some teenagers who need community service hours. They'll enjoy showing you their expertise and you'll be an old hand at Twitter in no time.

After you have a Twitter feed on your website, and you've let team leaders/staff members know the user name and password they need, you can sit back and let this particular social media function without much intervention, unless you have something to communicate to all of your members quickly and concisely.

QR Codes

One specific thing to mention that is Internet-based but can carry over into your print communication is QR (short for "quick response") codes. These are those scannable square black-and-white code blocks that

This QR code will take a user directly to the Enright CSA website when it is scanned

you see on posters and in ads all over the place these days. If someone with a smartphone or tablet scans the QR code, it will take them directly to your website.

Generate your own QR code at http://qrcode.kaywa.com and you can use it on brochures, business cards, posters, and displays to direct people to more information about your CSA.

These are just a few high-tech ways you can use to inform and connect with your CSA members and potential members. Though of course there's always the next big thing—as soon as it appears, you'll want to have a presence on it, too. In that sense, the online communications aspect of an urban CSA—or any other organization or business—can be a never-ending task. At some point, you just have to say "enough," turn off the computer, and go out in the field and start farming.

Index

crops
    planning spreadsheet for, 54–55
    selecting, 54–55
    planting charts, 53, 54–55, 98, 99, 100, 101
CSA. *see* Community-supported agriculture (CSA)
CSA management software, 84, 88
CSA policy statement, 86
    on website, 75
    for pickup, 70, 71

D

Dater Montessori School, Cincinnati, 15
delivery, of produce shares, 67
Department of Agriculture, U.S., 48
Detroit, urban agriculture in, 6, 16, 19
digital photographs, for website and blog images, 77
Direct Farm Ownership Loan Program, 27
discounts, for CSA membership, 31, 35
displays, to recruit members, 74, 80
distribution, 63–71
    finding space for, 24
drought, dealing with, 59
drought-resistant varieties, of produce, 60

E

early deposit, discount for, 35
Earthineer, 78
Edible Schoolyard Project, 17
emails, for communicating with members, 74, 76, 79
Enright Ridge CSA, 1, 2, 7, 12, 17, 23, 34, 38, 51, 92
    contact information, 8
Enright Ridge Urban EcoVillage (ERUEV), 1, 39, 40
entrepreneurial farmer CSA, 14
Excel worksheets, for CSA management, 88

F

Facebook, 30, 74, 75, 78, 107–108
family limited partnership, CSA as, 41
Farm Service Agency. *See* USDA Farm Service Agency (FSA)

farm subsidies, 48
farmers
    finding qualified, 41–42, 104–105
    interviewing, 104–105
    professional, 51
farmers' market, selling produce at, 67, 85
Farmigo (CSA management software), 88
farming. *See also specific types and methods of farming*
    backyard farming, 20–21
    finding land for, 19–23
    methods, intensive, 9
    urban CSA, 51–62
farmstand, selling produce at, 67, 85
fertility, of soil, 57
Field Guide for Beginning Farmers, 22
file extensions, for website and blog images, 77
financing for CSA, 39–49, 45–47
Findlay, General James, 17
Findlay Market, Cincinnati, 17, 18
Flickr, 107
flyers, 74, 79–80
food. *See also* local food movement
    long distance vs. locally grown, 30
food pantry, donating leftover produce to, 67
food-handling, classes in safe methods for, 69
French-intensive method of growing vegetables, 5
frequently asked questions, 87
    on website, 75
frost dates, 56
FSA. *See* USDA Farm Service Agency (FSA)
fundraising, 35

G

garden insurance, 47
garden teams, 44–45, 60
general partnership, CSA as, 41
Good Agricultural Practices (GAP), 25, 69–70
Good Handling Practices (GHP), 69–70
Google Docs, 88
Google Places, 107
Google+, 107
grants and grant writing, 35, 40, 46
Green Bean Delivery service, 18

Greenhorns' Field Guide for Beginning Farmers, 57
greenhouses, 23–24, 46, 55, 58
    maintenance of, 35
grocery stores, 48
    produce from, 5

H

harvesting produce, 61–62
health insurance, for CSA staff, 49
heavy metals, as soil toxins, 57
high-yield farming methods, 20
Hillside Community Garden, 15
hoop houses, 55, 58

I

institutional sales, of CSA produce, 85
insurance and liability issues, 47–49, 65
intensive farming methods, 9. *See also* French-intensive method of growing vegetables
intern system, to train new farmers, 48, 88, 90–91
interviewing, potential farmers, 41–42, 104–105
irrigation, 59–60. *See also* Water

J

Japan, communal agriculture in, 9
job creation, 91–92

L

labeling, produce, 68
labor issues, 90–91
land
    for farming, finding, 19–23, 46
    public, farming, 21–22
    purchasing, 22–23
    school district, for farming, 21
    semi-public, farming, 21–22
    vacant, farming 21
land trusts, farming land in, 21
late pickups, dealing with, 71
leasing land, methods for, 22
Leopold Center for Sustainable Agriculture, Iowa, 5
liability insurance, 47, 90
liability issues, for CSA, 47–49
limited liability company (LLC), CSA as, 41
limited partnership, CSA as, 41
local food movement, 18, 19, 31

Todmorden, Yorkshire, urban agriculture in, 16
tool shed, 59
tools, for farming, 46, 59
traceability, of contaminants in food, 69
training
  farm staff, 42–43
  farmers, 48, 88
  volunteers, 43–44
  work share members, 43–45, 60
trees, for perennial crops, 54
Twitter, using, 74, 108–109
  for scheduling work, 60
  widget for website, 108

U
unemployment insurance, for CSA staff, 49
United States, agriculture in, 9, 15
urban co-op farming method, 10. *See also* Co-op farms
urban CSA, starting, 4
urban farming, 1, 18
  in Buffalo, 19
  in Chicago, 6
  in Cincinnati, 8
  in Cleveland, 19
  compared to other types of CSAs, 2
  encouraging, 48–49
  in inner city neighborhoods, 27
  in Milwaukee, 6
  in New York City, 5
  in Paris, 5
  types of, 14–18

U.S. Department of Agriculture, and crop insurance, 48
USDA Farm Service Agency (FSA), 27
USDA regulations, for organic certification, 86

V
vacant land, for farming, finding, 21
value chains
  defined, 88
  establishing, 88–89
Victory Gardens, 5, 15
vineyards, urban, 14
Vista program, for CSA staffing, 90
volunteers
  members as, 34–35
  one-time, 43
  students as, 44
  training, 43–44

W
water, availability of, 25–26. *See also* Irrigation
Waters, Alice, School Lunch Initiative, 17
website, for CSA, 30, 75–76, 107
weed management, 60
wholesale sales, of CSA produce, 85
widgets, website, for social media, 108
Wikimedia Commons, images from, 77
Word-of-mouth advertising, for CSA, 30

WordPress, blog, 77
work hours
  form for, sample, 103
  posting on Twitter, 109
  tracking, 60
work share members, 91
  training, 43–45, 60
work shares, 34–35
  managing, 60–61
  scheduling work for, 44–45
workers' compensation, 49, 90
World War II Victory Gardens, 5, 15

Y
Yelp, 107
yield charts, 53
yield per acre, 10
  statistics for, 20
Yorkshire, England, urban agriculture in, 16
YouTube videos, 107

Z
zoning, 25

CPSIA information can be obtained
at www.ICGtesting.com
Printed in the USA
BVOW07s1128150616

452138BV00008B/41/P

9 780991 410705